The Face on the Screen

Death, Recognition and Spectatorship

Therese Davis

intellect™
Bristol, UK
Portland, OR, USA

First Published in the UK in 2004 by
Intellect Books, PO Box 862, Bristol BS99 1DE, UK

First Published in the USA in 2004 by
Intellect Books, ISBS, 920 NE 58th Ave. Suite 300, Portland, Oregon 97213-3786, USA

A catalogue record for this book is available from the British Library

ISBN 1-84150-084-4

Cover Design: Gabriel Solomons
Copy Editor: Holly Spradling

Printed and bound in Great Britain by Antony Rowe Ltd.

In this tender, haunting, imaginative, and innovative work, Therese Davis broadens and deepens cultural theory, away from a 1990s focus on mass culture as pleasure, towards an engagement in the new millennium with the image's darker powers: its capacity to reveal and engage with pain, illness, disease, blindness, trauma, death, mourning, loss, remembrance, melancholy. *The Face on the Screen* looks beyond the usual rush of the contemporary media's image-cultures which work to conceal the powers of death, to focus on moments – in medieval and baroque art, in a Proust 'scene', in photography, in film, in television – when a movement between recognition and becoming unrecognisable rehearses the experience of facing death itself, forces us to think of what lifelong we never wish to contemplate, our own death's head beneath our own faces. Davis evokes and discusses contemporary examples of images which shake us, which force upon us recognition of death's powers, images of Princess Diana's death and funeral, of dramatist Dennis Potter's posthumous reflections on screen, of actor Paul Eddington's disease-altered visage, of the shocking sight of the racist-defaced grave of Eddie Mabo whose name is forever associated with indigenous land rights in colonialist Australia, and of images of Ground Zero in New York's September 11. There is also a fascinating essay on the relationship between Charlie Chaplin's *City Lights* and early twentieth century research into blind people whose sight has been restored. As she explores these texts and events, Davis arranges conversations between some of the major theorists of modernity, engaging critically with Adorno, Levinas, Lacan, Deleuze and Guattari, while extending the insights of a range of thinkers she particularly admires: Schopenhauer, Simmel, Benjamin, Kracauer, De Man, Taussig. She makes journeys into unusual writings on physiognomy and blindness and face recognition. *The Face on the Screen* is as profound as it is poignant.

John Docker, Humanities Research Centre, Australian National University

Table of Contents

PreFace

The face counts for nothing in film unless it includes the death's head beneath.
— Siegfried Kracauer[i]

There was a time in screen culture when the face was a spectacular and mysterious image. Writing in the early part of the twentieth century, film theorist Béla Balázs claimed that cinematic close-ups of faces – gigantic 'severed heads', as he called them – constituted 'a new dimension, an entirely new mode of perception'.[i] In the image-cultures of contemporary media, however, the face is anything but mysterious. The 'talking head', for example, is the most banal unit in television's restricted syntax. In press photography, faces are over-used as obvious and clichéd expressions of so called universal human virtues and moral categories, while in the cinema the brilliance of the natural mobility of the human face has been eclipsed by the spectacle of computer-generated effects, such as morphing. In stark contrast to this wash of forgettable faces, there is the ever-changing, dazzling array of the faces of the famous. Although there is no mystery there either, for every famous face is accompanied by narratives of the procedures of making and unmaking celebrity.

In addition to the reduction of the face to a talking head and the commodification of any and all faces, media culture has also managed to make the sight of the faces of the dead and the dying banal. In the 1930s, photojournalists such as Robert Capa discovered that the most effective way to express the powers of death in photography is to get *close* to your subject. For Capa, this involved taking his Leica (lightweight) camera to European war zones and snapping pictures like his famous 'Death of a Republican Soldier' (1930).[ii] The immediacy of war expressed in photographs like Capa's brought a generation closer to death than they had ever been before. Yet, as we have come to know, mediated proximity to death does not necessarily lead to greater social understanding. Writing at approximately the same time that Capa was taking his photographs, Kracauer argued that the illustrated magazine is 'one of the most powerful means of organizing a strike against understanding'.[iii] In his view, 'the blizzard of photographs betrays an indifference toward what the things mean' (432). For Kracauer, the rise of the illustrated magazine in this period of mass death and destruction is itself 'a sign of *the fear of death*', 'an attempt to banish ... the recollection of death, which is part and parcel of every memory-image' (433). The cultural process of bombarding ourselves with images as a way of avoiding death's powers has continued through to the twenty-first century. In contemporary television, for example, instantaneous images of death have become institutionalized as the obligatory 'bang, bang' shot in nightly news reports of war, while the shock effect of close-up faces of death transmitted 'live' into our living rooms is parried by the sheer accumulation of such images. As Susan Buck-Morss and others convincingly argue, we have become *immune* to the sight of death – the endless CNN-style repetition of faces of the dead and dying has, to use Buck-Morss' term, 'anaesthetized' us to the shock of death.[iv] Well, most of the time.

1

I say most because one of the main aims of this book is to draw attention to the occasions in contemporary media when the face on the screen unexpectedly becomes a viable site for the transmission of death. This is not an argument about authenticity: the 'real' face versus its representation; actual death versus fictional accounts. Rather, my proposition is this: in order to discover the places in contemporary media where the face breaks through the anaesthetizing fog of the mediasphere to express death's powers we need to look beyond the immobilised faces of the dead to the places where the face becomes unrecognisable. For, as I show in the following chapters, the shock of recognition produced in the dialectic of recognition and unrecognisability *rehearses* the experience of facing death: those unexpected moments when we are suddenly made aware of the full powers of death: finality, irreversibility, absolute otherness.

At one moment in Milan Kundera's novel, *The Unbearable Lightness of Being*, for example, Tereza is looking at herself in the mirror. Kundera asserts that in this moment of reflection 'Tereza wonders what would happen if her nose were to grow a millimetre longer per day. How long would it take for her to become unrecognizable? And if her face no longer looked like Tereza, would Tereza still be Tereza?'[v] Standing before the mirror imagining incremental changes to the features of her face, Tereza sees her face anew, indeed, sees herself as *other* than who she knows herself to be. For Kundera, this experience of otherness engenders a feeling of wonderment: 'No wonderment at the immeasurable infinity of the soul', he writes. 'Rather, wonderment at the uncertain nature of the self and of its identity' (123). This is true. But it is also true to say that the image of a face becoming unrecognisable reveals more than the instability of the face as a representation of the self. It is also a vivid display of the way in which the face expresses the transient nature of human existence. In the projected image of her altered face, Tereza, like one of the medieval artist Hans Baldung's 'Maidens of Death' confronts the other, mortal face of self we spend our lives trying not to see. I suggest that we take this instance of a young woman confronting the image of her face becoming unrecognisable as a precise model of the viewing position that enables the face to become a viable site for the transmission of death in media culture. For just as Tereza's experience of seeing herself as unrecognisable reveals the transient nature of her existence, her vulnerability to change, so too faces on the screen can unexpectedly *turn* to reveal 'the *death's head* beneath', forcing us as spectators to recognise the full gravity of death's powers.

This approach to the face is indebted to Taussig's unique conception of defacement. In his study of public secrecy, *Defacement: Public Secrecy and the Labor of the Negative*, Taussig argues that acts of defacement unmask the mask of the face, exposing the secret of appearances as a dialectic of visibility and invisibility (2). His aim, as he states, is not to demystify the face. Rather, he is guided by Walter Benjamin's understanding of the search for truth as being 'not a matter of exposure which destroys the secret, but a revelation that does justice to it' (2). Here, I attempt to apply this insight into the face to the problem of mass mediatization of death and dying by showing how instances in film and television where the face reveals 'the *death's head* beneath' serve to expose the many ways in which the face is employed in screen media to conceal death, to *mask* its powers. As with Taussig, I do not wish to demystify the

2

face or, indeed, 'destroy' it, as philosophers Gilles Deleuze and Felix Guattari suggest we should aim to do.[vi] My aim is to examine how these moments in which we recognise the powers of death illuminate the underlining structures and logics of the image-cultures of contemporary media. In other words, I am interested in how faces on the screen unmask the screen itself *as* a face, indeed, as Kracauer suggests, a face of death.

This critical method is underpinned by Benjamin's theory of the image, in particular his notion of 'the dialectical image'. Benjamin's asserts that the dialectical image constitutes a specific viewing experience that he calls a moment of 'recognizability': an instance when it is possible to recognise the past as it flashes up in a fleeting image in the present only to disappear.[vii] He theorises that these dialectical collisions of past and present allow for political and historical consciousness, for in this instance the disappearing image of the past illuminates present forms of crisis and catastrophe. The use of Benjamin's philosophy to analyse faces on the screen as a dialectical image shifts the emphasis in discussion of death and media away from representation and ideology that posits media texts and journalists as the primary sites of meaning toward the spectator and processes of recognition and image-reception.[viii] In turn, this consideration of processes of recognition and 'recognizability' allows us to think about the face on the screen in terms other than identity and identification: namely, the face as a practice of the image that can enable social and historical consciousness.

The book begins with a close analysis of media reports of well-known British actor Paul Eddington's death from a rare skin cancer, which left him 'faceless' and unrecognisable. This chapter allows for the introduction of writers whose work is used throughout the book – Proust, Benjamin, and Kracauer – and raises key questions of recognition and spectatorship pursued in later chapters. The second chapter, 'Reading the Face', shifts the focus away from media culture to histories of methods for interpreting meaning in the face. It looks at how the classical 'science' of physiognomy has over the years served as a model for interpreting all sorts of surface phenomenon, paying particular attention to radical appropriations of this model by twentieth-century critical theorists, Theodor Adorno and Walter Benjamin.

Following on from these two chapters, the book begins a series of analyses of a diverse group of faces of death and the issues of recognition and spectatorship that arise in each. Chapter three, 'Severed Head', addresses the issue of immortality in the age of television as it is raised in the television event of the death of British screenwriter Dennis Potter. Here, I show how the figure of the severed head of a dead writer, which Potter employs as a device to connect his two final television drama series *turns* on the author to betray the inherent contradiction in his use of television as a vehicle for immortality. But, as I argue, this is a productive betrayal in the sense that it provides insight into the ways in which television serves as a site of public and private memory.

Chapter four examines the politics and trauma of non-recognition. This discussion is grounded in an analysis of the trope of defacement in the international award-winning biographical film, *Mabo: Life of an Island Man* (1997). I show how this film's attempt to make the face of the late Australian indigenous leader Eddie Mabo recognisable to the Australian public raises important questions about the trauma of legal non-recognition that continues to threaten reconciliation between indigenous and non-indigenous Australians.

Chapter five looks at the death of Princess Diana and the phenomenon of global recognition. Critical responses to the global outpourings of grief for Diana are loosely divided into two camps: the sociological view, in which the outpourings of grief are seen as a reflection of changing social values of death and a second, cynical view, which sees the phenomenon of collective grief as a symptom of a short-lived mass epidemic of hysteria. Sidestepping both of these positions, I examine the changing reception of Diana's globally recognisable face, arguing that her rapid transformation from media saint to forgotten princess reveals the logics of speed and politics of recognisability that underlie the image-cultures of contemporary media.

The relation between time, memory and recognisability is also of concern in the sixth chapter, 'Remembering the Dead: Faces of Ground Zero'. Here, I consider the implications of the terrorist attack on New York's World Trade Center towers as a *faceless* catastrophe. I argue that the replays of the attacks on New York and Washington dramatise a historically specific crisis in recognisability. I also show how this crisis underscores the cultural processes of memorialising the dead that frame the popular (and popularist) image of September 11.

Finally, chapter seven, 'First Sight', interweaves diverse visual and theoretical materials in a meditation on a certain kind of melancholy and trauma associated with the dialectic of recognition and unrecognisability. This involves bringing together early twentieth-century psychological studies of the recovery of sight by the congenitally blind with a series of famous close-ups from Charlie Chaplin's film *City Lights* (1930), in which a newly sighted flower girl fails to recognise the tramp as her one true love and with Benjamin's concept of the dialectical image, characterised as simultaneous blindness and illumination.

Throughout, I have attempted to write about the experience of recognising death in the dialectic of recognition and unrecognisability in such a way that it does not destroy the mysteriousness of the face. By this I do not mean that the face as a mystical or ecstatic image, in the sense that Roland Barthes suggests in his remarkable analysis of the face of Greta Garbo.[ix] Instead, I am once again guided by Benjamin when I seek the mysteriousness of the face in the socially charged world of bodies and things. As Benjamin once wrote: 'we penetrate the mystery only to the degree that we recognize it in the everyday world, by virtue of a dialectical optic that perceives the everyday as impenetrable, the impenetrable as everyday.[x] In the following chapters I take this understanding of mysteriousness as the starting point for my discussion of occasions in media culture when an image of a face becoming unrecognisable makes death visible.

In the early stages of my research on this topic, I was fortunate to participate in two separate international seminars at the University of Newcastle. The first was led by Michael Taussig and the second by Miriam Hansen. In their different ways, both seminars provided me with the opportunity to develop my understanding of Walter Benjamin's writings. I am very grateful to both Miriam Hansen and Michael Taussig for this opportunity, as well as their invaluable feedback on early versions of chapters one and four. I am especially grateful to Jane Goodall, who mentored me throughout the process of researching this book and who encouraged me, in the full sense of the word, to experiment with different modes of academic writing. Jodi Brooks is one of the most intellectually generous people I know. I am extraordinarily grateful for her support and interest in my work. In addition, there is a list of other wonderful friends, colleagues and students who supported me in the writing of this book and to whom I am very much indebted. This list includes: David Boyd, Felicity Collins, Linda Connor, John Docker, Philip Dwyer, John Gillies, Chris Healy, Minae Inahara, Ivor Indyk, Suzanne Johnson, Anthony McCosker, Helen Macallan, Dianne Osland, Cassi Plate, Mark Prince, Pam Robertson, Kathy Robinson, David Rowe, Linnell Secomb, Ros Smith and Peter Williams. I am also extremely grateful for the support I received from my family. During the period of writing this book my family experienced what seemed to me to be an unfair share of serious illness and death. There were many times when I didn't want to continue writing. Not because there is a direct relationship between my personal experience of loss and grief and the subject of this book. On the contrary, if I have come to know anything about death it is the terrible cost of making it generalizable. And it is precisely this gap between the particularity of death – the acute sense of the finality and absolute irreversibility of death we feel when a loved one dies – and the generalization of death that occurs in the image-cultures of contemporary media that I want to draw attention to in the analyses of faces throughout. This book is for my family, especially my parents, my gorgeous daughter Grace, who has lived with this project for more than half her life, and Samantha, who died far too young and who is missed every day.

ENDNOTES

[i] Béla Balázs, Theory of the Film: Character and Growth of a New Art, trans. Edith Bone (New York: Dover Publications, 1970), 60.

[ii] Robert Capa, *Robert Capa*, trans. Abigail Pollock (New York: Pantheon, 1989), 73.

[iii] Siegfried Kracauer, 'Photography', trans. Thomas Y. Levin, *Critical Inquiry*, 19 (1993), 432.

[iv] Susan Buck-Morss, 'Aesthetics and Anaesthetics: Walter Benjamin's Artwork Essay Reconsidered', *October* 62 (1992). Also see Lynne Kirby, 'Death and the Photographic Body', *Fugitive Images: from Photography to Video*, ed. Patrice Petro (Bloomington and Indianapolis: Indiana University Press, 1995); Mary Anne Doane, 'Information, Crisis, Catastrophe', in *Logics of Television*, ed. Patricia Mellencamp (London: British Film Institute, 1990); Patricia Mellencamp, 'TV Time and Catastrophe or Beyond the Pleasure Principle of Television', in *Logics of Television*, 1990.

[v] Milan Kundera, 'Conversation with Milan Kundera on the Art of the Novel', trans. Linda Asher, *Salmagundi*, 73 (1987), 123.

[vi] See Gilles Deleuze and Felix Guattari's 'Faciality: Ground Zero' in *A Thousand Plateaus: Capitalism and Schizophrenia*, trans. Brain Massumi (Minneapolis: Minnesota University Press, 1987).

[vii] Walter Benjamin, '"N" (Re: the Theory of Knowledge, Theory of Progress)',

trans. Leigh Hafrey and Richard Sieburth, *Benjamin: Philosophy, Aesthetics, History*, ed. Gary Smith, (Chicago: University of Chicago Press, 1989), 50.

[viii] For example, see Susan D. Moeller, *Compassion Fatigue: How the Media Sell Disease, Famine, War and Death* (London and New York: Routledge, 1998).

[ix] Roland Barthes, 'The Face of Garbo', *Mythologies*, trans. Annette Lavers (London: Paladin, 1973).

[x] Walter Benjamin, 'Surrealism', *Reflections, Essays, Aphorisms, Autobiographical Writings*, ed. Peter Demetz, trans. Edmund Jephcott (New York: Schoken, 1986), 189-190.

Video enlargement from Face to Face *(Author's Collection)*

Chapter 1

Becoming Unrecognisable

I remember staying up through the night to watch CNN's live coverage of Yitzhak Rabin's burial service and how it was a speech given by his granddaughter at that event which brought me closest to the significance of his death.[i] The granddaughter explained to the world watching that the memorialising images of Rabin's face was not the face she knew. This was not her grandfather we saw on the screen. On the contrary, in death Rabin was, for her, unrecognisable – 'a smile that is no longer'. While Western news services desperately tried to sustain Rabin's recognisability, to allow viewers to *continue* to see him 'as he was' – indeed, to allow the dead to speak again through his last public words uttered at a peace rally only minutes before he was killed – it was also reported that British actor, Paul Eddington, best known for roles he played in BBC (UK) comedies *Yes, Minister* and *Yes, Prime Minister*, died of a rare skin cancer which left him 'faceless' and 'unrecognisable'. While I make no attempt now to compare these disparate stories, it was the tension produced in the strangeness of these two faces coming together, back to back, as they did in many of the Australian television news broadcasts, that got me thinking in a new way about the face and death and the problems of recognition and recognisability.[ii]

What I saw that night after Rabin's assassination as I was switching between various news services was that just as reports on Rabin sought to restore his face in death, television news tried equally hard to smooth over the shock of Eddington's facelessness in life. For Rabin's granddaughter, the mass circulation of her grandfather's image was unbearable. Addressing her dead grandfather, she cried: 'The television does not stop transmitting your picture'. Yet, it was not these pictures that news services identified as potentially 'disturbing' but the image of Paul Eddington's apparent facelessness. In this chapter, I explore what it means to look directly into Eddington's face, to look in the way television advised us not to. For as with the strange mix of tenses in Rabin's granddaughter's speech, this direct view of the spectacular loss of Eddington's well-known face shatters the illusion of eternal sameness – the almost sacred conception in Western cultures of a unitary, transcendent self. And as I will show, to see through this particular veil is to look in the way that Maurice Blanchot suggests Orpheus did when he 'turned back': 'to look into the night at what the night is concealing – the other night, concealment which becomes visible'.[iii] Or, in this case, to look into the face at what the face normally conceals – 'the blinding non-existence of death', which our hearts, as Schopenhauer once said, tell us cannot possibly be true.[iv]

I: When People See People

Channel Ten (Australia) reported on Paul Eddington's death by showing three short grabs – two of which were images of him as he had not been seen on television before.[v] The first was taken from the long running British television series *Yes, Prime Minister*, which made Eddington internationally recognisable as the face of Jim Hacker, Minister of Parliament. Here, Hacker explains: *If people saw people coming, before people saw them seeing people coming, people would see people.* This instance of 'Hackeresque' logic, underscored by the laughter track, becomes uncanny when this image, serving now to stand in for Eddington, cuts to the second image, a wide shot of an unrecognisable figure. Although Eddington is seen in this second shot in conversation, his voice has been muted, replaced by the voice of the news reader who reports: *Of course, that's how most people remember Eddington – the bumbling MP, star of the TV comedy series 'Yes, Prime Minister'. But at the end he was almost unrecognisable – his skin blotchy and his hair falling out.* The report then cuts to a final close-up shot of Eddington's silent, unrecognisable face. The reader concludes: *He was suffering from a rare skin disease, which probably cost him his life.*

Ten's story attempted to compensate for the shock of Eddington's apparently sudden unrecognisability by projecting on to him an image not simply of a former self but a fictional self. Eddington speaks not as himself, that is, as actor, but as character. It would seem that Ten preferred to confer on to Eddington a fixed, fictional identity, to have him speak from the grave as another, rather than face the mystery of his facelessness, or, worse, perhaps, allow for a faceless figure to speak. Not that I'm suggesting Ten's effort should be deplored. While their 'before and after' approach may be regarded as somewhat tacky, so called tasteful approaches taken by some other news services, such as ABC (Australia), for example, were equally problematic. Tip-toeing around the subject of his disfigurement by showing him *only* in character, the ABC spoke of Eddington's facelessness in the hushed, holy tones of tragedy. Descriptions of the effects of skin cancer as a tragic situation were, I am sure, intended to give some kind of 'deeper' significance to this disconcerting calamity. But in an interview shown on Australian television a week or so after the above-mentioned news report, Eddington describes his condition in very different terms, referring to it as an 'absurd situation' and claiming that the look of his face is nothing less than 'grotesque'.

The grotesque is most easily defined as an un-natural excess. The grotesque face is overblown and distorted: it is an exaggeration of the face. What shocks us into the repulsive/attractive gaze of the grotesque, 'the embarrassed smile', as Wolfgang Kayser puts it, is the recognition of a resemblance to, or continuity between, the human form and other forms, such as animal or plant forms, or even other forms of pictorial representation.[vi] In a chapter of his influential book on the topic where he attempts to define the specific affect of the grotesque, Kayser writes: 'We are so strongly affected and terrified because it is our world which ceases to be reliable, and we feel that we would be unable to live in this changed world. The grotesque instils fear of life rather than fear of death' (185). However, in Ten's report Eddington's altered face appeared to be neither deformed nor misshapen. It did not appear overblown, nor was there any trace of animality. What appeared on the screen was a perfectly proportional face altered only at surface level – it was, to put it bluntly, a peculiarly blank face, non-descript in the way that police identikit pictures resemble faces in general but no one face in particular. Perhaps then even a term like 'the grotesque' is too general when speaking about this face, because it does not distinguish between the excessive *facedness* of deformity and the baffling *facelessness* of Eddington's sudden unrecognisability.

As if erased, Eddington's face was not so much 'monstrous', as the term grotesque suggests, but rather, quite simply, a face *without resemblance*, in the sense that it bore no resemblance to his former look or to any face in particular. In terms of the grotesque, disfigurement of this kind – that is, a situation in which all the unique lines, forms and textures of the face are *effaced* – is excessive to the degree that it makes visible a face which is a pure abstraction of face – sur*face*. To see the face in this way, that is, as a face never seen before, brings us closer, perhaps, to the fear it instils. As Kayser says, not so much a fear of death itself, but of the uncertainties of life. Or to put it slightly differently, a face becoming unrecognisable is not of the order of the fantastic but very much of this world – the visceral, the bodily, and the social.

Clearly, the unrecognisability of Eddington's face that instils in viewers a fear of the contingencies of life constitutes a shock experience. In this way, less extreme or lasting forms of faces becoming unrecognisable might also be considered to have a similar effect. Take, for example, those everyday fleeting moments of alienation when a face we know well, the face of a lover or a child – a most adored and searched-into-and-over face – *changes* before our eyes. Australian artist, Joy Hester, once described these moments as, 'that fleeting mobile moment in which one sees for the first time the person and this "first" time appears all the time in Gray's (her lover's(face'.[vii] As encounters with absolute difference, the shock of a face becoming unrecognisable suspends us in the dark, where we grasp for impossible resemblances.

The idea of the face as an encounter with difference is central to Emmanuel Levinas' philosophy of ethics. In 'Ethics as First Philosophy', Levinas asserts that the experience of coming face to face with another is the primary experience of existence. He argues that becoming 'I' involves first facing up to responsibility for the Other: 'Responsibility for the Other, for the naked face of the first individual to come along, a responsibility that goes beyond what I may or may not have done to the Other, whatever act I may or may not have committed, as if I were devoted to the other before being devoted to myself. Or more exactly, as if I had to answer for the other's death even before being'.[viii] For Levinas, the relation of face-to-faceness constitutes a unique experience in which we recognise not that we live because the other dies, but that we live *only* to recognise the Other's death. This recognition is possible, he argues, because of the transcendence of the face. In his essay, *Totality and Infinity*, he contends that sensations can create qualities that do not require cognizance.[ix] Or, as he puts it, 'qualities without support' (188). He writes: 'sensation recovers a "reality" when we see in it not the subjective counterpart of objective qualities, but an enjoyment "anterior" to the crystallisation of consciousness, I and not-I, into subject and object. This crystallisation occurs not as the ultimate finality of enjoyment but as a moment of its becoming, to be interpreted in terms of enjoyment' (188). For Levinas, the only given in the delirious space of pure sensation is the face. The face cuts through or transcends the nothingness of the sensual world, opening up what he describes as 'the infinite relation' of face-to-faceness, which, in his view, recovers a reality that takes us beyond totalising thinking. In this way, the experience of the infinite – a space 'without proportion', as he sees it – gives rise to the secret language of the face: the demand by the face that we respond to it cancels the eyes: we respond to *the call* of the Other, which speaks through the secret language of the face.[x]

Another way of putting this is that in Levinas' philosophy, recognition of death in the face of the other 'dazzles' the self. Blinded, the self passively subordinates its existence to the other. Hence, recognition of death in the face of the other is first and foremost an ethical experience. But does this philosophy of ethics help us to understand the viewing experience of recognising death in the dialectic of recognition and unrecognisability set off in media reports of Paul Eddington's facelessness? And exactly what would that mean in terms of the apprehension of the face as a form of vision? Certainly, it is true to say that when first confronted by the close-up detail of Eddington's altered face I experienced a sense of the infinite of indeterminacy. But I cannot say that this experience led to 'a call of the Other' that took me outside of historical time. To the contrary, for me this image enabled a very specific recognition of time past. Confronted by an image of facelessness, I found myself unable to not look. I was drawn to Eddington's otherness with the same awe and amazement that I had once experienced before illustrations of flayed anatomical faces in my grandfather's leather-bound *Book of Disease and Physiology*. Yet, while the strange (*'estranging'*) objectivity of Eddington's facelessness made it impossible to find resemblance between this face before me and images of Eddington imprinted in my consciousness, my response was neither one of horror nor disgust. Rather, I found myself thinking quite specifically about my grandfather dying of emphysema, his cheekbones protruding through his skin like scars. Looking into my grandfather's face, I had been prodded by death for the first time. Although I was only seven years old I had understood completely the meaning of what I had seen. As with Rabin's granddaughter, perhaps, I knew I had seen my grandfather's face for the last time. It's not that Eddington's face resembled my grandfather's, but rather that the shock of Eddington's facelessness *renewed* in me a very specific, forgotten childhood experience of mortality. In other words, the indeterminacy revealed in the sight of a face becoming unrecognisable 'exposed' – like some lost photographic negative – a final image of my grandfather's face imprinted within me in some deep, unconscious way. And for this reason, I would describe the viewing experience not in terms of the eternal time of Levinas' ethics but rather as a shock of recognition that enables consciousness of what Benjamin calls 'missed experience', a sensation akin to Proust's notion of the *mémoire involontaire*.[xi]

There is a section of Siegfried Kracauer's *Theory of Film – The Redemption of Physical Reality* where he associates the objectivity of the photographic nature of film with Proust's notion of *mémoire involontaire*.[xii] Here, Kracauer quotes a long passage from Proust's *Remembrance of Things Past*, in which the narrator enters a room in which his grandmother is seated and, remaining unnoticed, sees for the first time that she has aged:

I was in the room, or rather I was not yet in the room since she was not aware of my presence ... Of myself ... there was present only the witness, the observer with a hat and travelling coat, the stranger who does not belong to the house, the photographer who has called to take a photograph of places which one will never see again. The process that mechanically occurred in my eyes when I caught sight of my grandmother was indeed a photograph. We never see the people who are dear to us save in the animated system, the perpetual motion of our incessant love for them, which before allowing the images that their faces present to reach us catches them in a vortex, flings them back upon the idea that we have always had of them, makes them adhere to it, coincide with it. How, since into the forehead, the cheeks of my grandmother I had been accustomed to read all the most delicate, the most permanent qualities of her mind; how, since every casual glance is an act of necromancy, each face that we love a mirror of the past, how could I have failed to overlook what in her had become dulled and changed, seeing that in the most trivial spectacles of our daily life our eye charged with thought, neglects, as would a classical tragedy, every image that does not assist the action of the play and retains only those that may help to make its purpose intelligible ... I, for whom my grandmother was still myself, I who had never seen her save in my own soul, always in the same place in the past, through the transparent sheets of contiguous, overlapping memories, suddenly in our drawing room which formed part of *a new world, that of time,* saw, sitting on the sofa, beneath the lamp, red-faced, heavy and common, sick, lost in thought, following the lines of a book with eyes that seemed hardly sane, a dejected old woman whom I did not know. (14) (My emphasis)

In this evocative passage, Proust compares the narrator who sees his grandmother with a newly acquired objectivity to a photographer: seen photographically the grandmother appears to the narrator as an unrecognisable 'stranger'. More than this, the grandmother's unrecognisability effaces the narrator's loving memory of her. He is thrust into a new viewing position: a photographic viewpoint, in which she appears, 'red-faced, heavy and common, sick, lost in thought, following the lines of a book with eyes that seemed hardly sane, a dejected old woman ...' There are of course a number ways to read this scene. On one hand, this description is charged with sexual difference: it is a kind of primal scene that reveals a history of men's idealisation of woman. The narrator is crushed when he sees his grandmother for the first time in her mortal state. Putting this question of gender to one side, we can also see that this is a scene of self-knowledge, for it is not only the grandmother who is transformed in the narrator's experience of unrecognisability. We learn that the experience of seeing his grandmother 'photographically' also transforms the narrator: he too becomes a stranger in his own home – 'an observer with a hat and travelling coat'. The shocking sight of his grandmother's aging takes the narrator out of the comfortable space of the home and transports him into what he calls, 'a new world, that of time'. If, as Kracauer suggests, for Proust, 'photography is the product of complete alienation' (15), then this alienation is also always a temporal experience – a shock experience in which the narrator finds himself caught between past and present, a temporality similar to the stilled or suspended state of the awareness of mortality we commonly refer to as 'facing death'.

Leading on from Proust's insight into unrecognisability and Kracauer's use of it for his theory of film, it could be said that my experience of the objectivity of Eddington's facelessness enabled in me, and, surely, others, a different kind of recognition. This form of recognition is not a psychological identification with the screen subject, which would in fact be misrecognition of self. Rather, it takes the form of a perception of change that constitutes an experience of seeing *as if* for the first time, an experience that takes us beyond cognitive recognition, opening our eyes to what Kracauer calls 'crude existence'(19). Kracauer discusses how photography tends to stress the fortuitous, the unexpected: 'even the most typical portraits' he writes, 'must retain an accidental character – as if they were plucked en route and still quivered with crude existence' (19). Confronted by this crude existence we are made aware of life's contingencies. And in this sense we could say that the 'crude existence' transmitted by the nakedness of Eddington's face unsettles the certainty of eternal sameness and recognisability. Thus, here also, it is not only the other who is changed by the trauma of unrecognisability, for this experience forces the viewer to see him or herself differently. Indeed, it is possible, as it was for me, to remember oneself anew in the light of a hitherto forgotten trauma of the unrecognisability of death.

By smoothing over the shock of Eddington's facelessness in life through the so-called restoration of his former face, Channel Ten's crude juxtapositions revealed what is usually concealed – that is, the contingency of identity. Before unrecognisability the viewer is suspended between the familiar and the strange, the known and the unknowable. And just as unrecognisability reveals the mortal nature of human existence, its affect can be best understood in terms of the self-estranging affect of loss and death. The shock of unrecognisability is thus an affect not dissimilar to that sudden realisation of the loss of a loved one, a shock that hits like a blow to the head, emptying us of all life's meaning, a feeling that passes through us as a giant unstoppable shudder, leaving us naked and exposed, strangers to ourselves in 'a new world, that of time'.

II: The Underside of the Mask

A week or so after the news reports on Paul Eddington's death, ABC TV (Australia) broadcast a special edition of the BBC series *Face to Face* featuring an hour-long interview with Eddington. In this interview, recorded a short time prior to his death and shot entirely in close-up, Eddington was asked how he found the courage to appear 'as himself', meaning in his then current state of disfigurement. He said that he drew on his training as an actor. Bracing himself as one might don a mask; Eddington faced others around him as an actor faces an audience. Ironically, only in this state of otherness could Eddington become himself, and as himself, he could not perform being other than himself. Invoking Roland Barthes' sense of the mask, it can be said that Eddington's face had become a mask proper. As Barthes says, 'The mask is the meaning insofar as it is absolutely pure (as it was in ancient theatre.)'[xiii] And in this case, Eddington's 'pure' (or absolute) otherness exposes the representational practices of the face used in dramatic film as the masks they are. As he explained it, he was no longer able to act the roles he had previously performed: *I was asked by a producer to do a film and I said, "Well we haven't met for some time, oughtn't you come and have a look at me" ... I said "Let's have a make-up test, a film test," and we did. She wrote a regretful letter saying, "I'm sorry it's a major part and the cameras simply won't be able to come in close enough."*

In *Theory of Film* Kracauer argues that there are two ways of approaching the face in close-up: as 'a unit of montage' and as 'an end in itself'.[xiv] As a unit of montage, the close-up face is a *sign* that points to other objects around it. Through the technique of cross-cutting between the face and other objects, film can create sympathies and inner thoughts. Through these kinds of techniques film creates an illusionary subjectivity. By allowing us to seemingly penetrate the mind of the character via the face, to see as the character sees, film invites audiences to identify with the screen subject. In this *representational* approach to the close-up, the face is seen as a means to an inner self, an illusion of a unitary self, which Eddington's pure otherness would have of course shattered. Given the dominance of representational practices of the face, Eddington found himself 'typecast'. As he put it: [t]*he BBC asked me to do Henry V playing Justice Shallow. I said, "I do look grotesque you know ..." They said, "No, no, that's what we want." Perhaps a revival of the Elephant Man or the Man in the Iron Mask I could manage, but apart from that I shall have to confine myself to radio.*

It is interesting that on radio, the recognisability of Eddington's voice offset the face, while on television, the severity of his altered face quite literally de-faces his voice and proper name: on television Eddington appears as an impostor. Hence, from around this time, Eddington performed only on radio, apart from some interviews for TV conducted shortly before his death. And it is in one of those interviews – a profile in the series *Face to Face* – that another kind of closeness is enabled. Discussing the second approach to the close-up, Kracauer asks if the close-up face can ever be that which the viewing subject 'simply passes through and beyond' to other things, to other shots around it (47). He suggests that the close-up face can also be seen as 'an end in itself' (48). In terms of recognisability, the cinematic face can be read-off as a set of expressions of personality, a sign of an inner self or guide to inner thoughts. But film also makes the face perceptible as sur*face*. That is to say, the face can be recognised in film in its purely physical form.

Citing the example of a close-up of Mae West's hands in D.W. Griffith's film *Intolerance*, Kracauer claims there is no doubt that the purpose of the image is to 'impress upon us her inner condition'(47). However, as he adds, this is not the only way to experience the image: '... besides making us experience what we would in a measure have experienced anyway because of our familiarity with the characters involved, this close-up contributes something momentous and unique – it reveals how hands behave under the impact of utter despair' (47). For Kracauer, film can re-open spectator's eyes to physical reality, that is, the material world. This aspect of film is crucial for, as he puts it, it leads us through 'the thicket of material life from which they [the emotional and intellectual concepts which comprise the film's plot] emerge and in which they are embedded' (48). It is also this notion of physical embeddedness that leads us to an understanding of the close-up as that which can set forth in spectator's series of unconscious memories and associations. Inviting us to enter a wholly different realm of subject-object relations, Kracauer invokes Walter Benjamin's idea of the 'optical unconscious'. Quoting Benjamin in 'The Work of Art in the Age of Mechanical Reproduction', Kracauer argues that close-up images, '"blow up our environment in a double sense: they enlarge it literally; and in doing so, they blast the prison of conventional reality, opening up expanses which we have explored at best in dreams before"'(48).[xv]

Benjamin introduced the idea of the camera as unleashing an optical unconscious in his 1931 essay, 'A Small History of Photography'.[xvi] In this essay, Benjamin writes how from its inception, photography was criticised on the grounds that not only was it impossible for a human countenance to be captured by a machine, but that the wish to do so was 'blasphemous' (241). He argues that rather than compare the new technology of the camera with past art forms, such as painting, it is better to instead focus on the specificity of the new, 'profane' mode of perception generated by the camera. Benjamin and Kracauer share the view that photography and film bring the world closer to viewers only to put them at a distance from what they see by revealing the world in its alienated form. In his essay on photography, Benjamin describes a photograph by Octavius Hill. He writes: '[I]n Hill's Newhaven fishwife, her eyes cast down in such indolent, seductive modesty, there remains something that goes beyond testimony to the photographer's art, something that cannot be silenced, that fills you with an unruly desire to know what her name was, the woman who was alive there, who even now is still real and will never consent to be wholly absorbed in art' (242-243).

This is not an argument for photographic realism. What Benjamin opens up here for discussion in this description is the peculiar temporal dimension of the reception of photography. He suggests that the photograph captures a past moment. This process is not a matter of freezing the moment like some 'memento mori' – the 'That-has-been', as Barthes puts it.[xvii] For Benjamin, photography is an aesthetic experience in which the recognition of the collision of the past and present creates a new mode of perception. He concludes thus:

> ... the most precise technology can give its products a magical value, such as a painted picture can never have for us. No matter how artful the photographer, no matter how carefully posed his subject, the beholder feels an irresistible urge to search a picture for a tiny spark of contingency, of the Here and Now, with which reality has so to speak seared the subject, to find the inconspicuous spot where in the immediacy of the long forgotten moment the future subsists so eloquently that we, looking back, may rediscover it. For it is another nature that speaks to the camera than to the eye: other in the sense that a space informed by human consciousness gives way to a space informed by the unconscious (243).

From this observation, Benjamin goes on to develop his idea of the unconscious optics of the camera, that is, a way of seeing that is not available to the naked eye. He writes:

It is through photography that we first discover the existence of this optical unconscious, just as we discover the instinctual unconscious through psychoanalysis ... photography reveals ... the physiognomic aspects of visual worlds which dwell in the smallest things, meaningful and yet covert enough to find a hiding place in waking dreams, but which, enlarged and capable of formulation, make the difference between technology and magic visible as a thoroughly historical variable (243-244).

As with Benjamin, Kracauer was attracted to the capacity of both photography and film to reveal historical contingencies. In her essay on Kracauer's material aesthetic of film, Miriam Hansen reminds us that Kracauer too wrote an essay on photography, some four years prior to Benjamin's piece, and that in his essay he raises the significance of the specific temporality of the photographic experience.[xviii] Hansen goes on to explain that Benjamin and Kracauer hold similar views to photography and film: '... Kracauer shares with Benjamin the notion of shock ...' (459). She writes, 'It could be argued that *Theory of Film* was designed to resume the allegorical vision of Benjamin's tragedy book, its implicit analysis of modernity as the petrified, frozen landscape of history' (444). However, for Hansen, the significant difference between the views held by these two theorists is that while Benjamin sees photography and film as media that can redeem the long-past moment seared in the image for the present, Kracauer theorises a different form of recognition. Hansen writes: 'For Kracauer, less overtly messianic than his friend, the breeze of the future that makes the beholder shudder is that of his own material contingency' (455). She quotes Kracauer: '"Those things once clung to us like our skin, and this is how our property still clings to us today. We are contained in nothing and photography assembles fragments around a nothing"' (455-456). For Kracauer, photography not only constitutes a new kind of temporal experience that makes historical contingencies visible, but it is also a new way of encountering mortality. In Kracauer's words: 'an awareness of a history that does not include us' (456). Here, I am not so much concerned with Hansen's argument about significant differences between Kracauer's theory of the image and Benjamin's, but rather I focus on the ways in which both viewpoints lead to an understanding of the shock of non-identity as an aesthetic experience that creates a consciousness of time.

When Kracauer writes that 'The face counts for nothing in film unless it includes the *death's head* beneath' he invokes Benjamin's study into the German allegorical poets use of the death's head as an allegorical symbol of history. For Kracauer, the inherent strangeness or otherness of the face seen in close-up reveals the inherent transience of human nature and thus, to use Hansen's words, 'deflate(s) the image of the sovereign individual'.[xix] In the *danse macabre*, death is figured as a faceless skeleton, descending upon unsuspecting individuals in the course of their daily activities: a lord on his rounds of his property, a worker in the field. But as cultural critics have noted, the function of this motif is more than a visual reminder of mortality.[xx] The 'death's head' is a complex and ironic practice of the image that expresses what Sarah Goodwin describes as 'the indifference of indifference'. For Kracauer, film has the capacity to show the presence of death in life in a similar way. He is not here referring to clichéd images of the corpse or the fantastic film effects that bring us animated skeletons. Rather, he is, I believe, concerned with moments in film where we become not only aware of mortality but the indifference of death to forms of social organisation. In Kracauer's analysis of the significance of the shot of Mae West's hand, for example, he proposes what Hansen describes as 'a material aesthetic of film' in which the visible frailty and permeability of the body reveals the contingencies of life and the inherent transitoriness of human existence, a sensation that cuts across narrative considerations. As with Benjamin's notion of the optical unconscious, which, he argues, makes 'physiognomical aspects of the world visible', Kracauer insists the face is able to make this knowledge visible in moments where the senses are engaged – '(film) addresses the viewer as "a corporeal human being"; it seizes the "human being with skin and hair"'.[xxi] In this way, film carries social knowledge not only at the level of narrative – that is, in and through narrative techniques, such as plot and characterisation. It also reveals social reality through its powerful appeal to the senses.

From this perspective, it is possible to see that not only is there a similarity of effect between the close-up and the image of a face becoming unrecognisable, but there is also a *reciprocity*: The close-up generates the physical affect of non-identity, and in turn, the face becoming unrecognisable brings into focus the affective power of the close-up mostly overlooked in the reduced dimensions of contemporary screen forms such as television. In television culture, the talking head is the most banal unit of visual language. The bare-facedness of faces becoming unrecognisable – as an image of irrevocable loss of face, in the case of Eddington's de-facement, or, more generally, as the shock of the changeability of all faces – brings to the small screen something of the powerful, 'silent' language of early cinema faces. Most important, it reveals the contingencies of life and, as both Benjamin and Kracauer suggest, it does this by awakening viewers through its powerful shock to the senses.

Returning to the interview with Eddington we find that although the relentless close-ups of Eddington's unrecognisable face in *Face to Face* take us doubly close to the face, this is not a closeness that invites us to penetrate it. On the contrary, as a viewer I found myself captive to the physical strangeness of the face, an effect similar, perhaps, to that created by the first close-up faces of early cinema, the 'gigantic "severed heads"' which, film theorist Balázs claims constitutes 'a new dimension'.[xxii] In the enlarging perspective of a face becoming unrecognisable it is possible to see, for example, the minute details of the movements of the face usually overlooked in television. In *Face to Face* there is an unsettling moment when Eddington, describing how his children call him every day, falters. In this fleeting second we can witness the extreme *pressure* of becoming unrecognisable as Eddington, suddenly distracted and confused, mistakenly says that when his children call, they ask him 'who' he is (rather than 'how' he is.) I am not suggesting that this slip of the tongue, doubly amplified in a painful, anxious look that crosses his face, *exposes* the 'real' Eddington, opposed to some other, 'false' impression.[xxiii] Just as the viewer can take this slip of the tongue as an unconscious expression of his feelings about becoming unrecognisable, so too his face can be seen to unconsciously reveal what cannot be said, what is too painful or, indeed, impossible, to express directly.

In the final moments of the interview Eddington is asked by the interviewer how he would like to be remembered. Shown in profile and in extreme close-up, Eddington says, 'Well', takes a long breath and pauses. Perhaps he is conscious of how he is about to repeat already rehearsed lines, for he says: *I've said this at the end of my book. And it sounds mock modest, but it's not, if you think about it. You see, a journalist once asked me, what would I like my epitaph to be, and I said I would like it to be, 'He did very little harm'.* At this point Eddington pauses again before he continues: *That's not easy.* The programme then cuts to an extreme close-up of his full face as he concludes: *Most people seem to me to do a great deal of harm. If I could be remembered as doing very little, that would suit me.* On one level there is an absolutely predictable closure in Eddington's effortless performance of the last line of the interview. An act of self-commemoration, Eddington speaks as the already dead. Yet, on another level, a tele*visual* level, it can be noticed that as these words are spoken, as his mouth is set in place, as his head makes a steady, purposeful nod and his eyes gently open and close, his face reveals nothing of 'who he was', but something of the indeterminacy of self he proposes in his request to be remembered for 'what he was not'.

In visual terms, this kind productive negativity can be performed not only as a censure but as a stripping back of the subject (as opposed to a building up.) And this is, I argue, the performance mode perfected by Eddington in both this final interview and in his most well-known role of Hacker in the popular comedy series, *Yes, Minister* and *Yes, Prime Minister*. The fictional role of Hacker required Eddington to perform in a light-handed manner, that is, in a manner diametrically opposed to the heavier role of his fictional assistant Humphrey who is the personification of cynicism. As the 'bumbling MP', Hacker is true to his name, for his constant stream of non-sequiturs serve to undercut the weighty language of cynicism and thus, in a negative, although, as I say, light-handed way, subvert the language of rationalism.[xxiv] In his final interview, Eddington performs another version of this form of negativity as he *doubly* addresses viewers: what is seen *before* the obvious 'brave face' – and here I especially want to stress both the spatial and temporal aspects of beforeness – is the emergence of another 'invisible' face, as Balázs calls it (76). This is not some kind of true face of self hidden behind the mask of performance. Rather, this second face enacts a kind of crosstalk or doublespeak. One face performs while the other signals to spectators that the actor is aware of being observed, while never giving away the act that requires him to appear unaware.[xxv] Or, as Hacker put it: *If people saw people coming, before people saw them seeing people coming, people would see people...*

Acknowledging the performativeness of this televisual moment opens the way for us to see the look Eddington signals as a *double look*. It is also a look that opens up the possibility for viewers of what Benjamin calls 'double insight'. Here, it is possible to see the way in which the face draws us into a particular spatio-temporal relation to the other, the way in which the face can make felt what cannot be seen – in this case, the material event of death, the loss of Paul Eddington's life, smoothed over and concealed in the endless 'repeats' of his series. Here, in this moment, past, present and future collide in an image of Eddington reflecting on his past, while, at the same time looking blindly into a future in which he will no longer exist. This is in fact an interlocking of blind gazes, for to see Eddington *not seeing us*, is surely to recognise what Schopenhauer means by 'the blinding image of non-existence'. And in this way, Eddington's final performance is neither simply a self-commemoration – an immortalising image of a past self – nor a mirror image of the viewer's mortality. It is, I suggest, an infinitely present *rehearsal* of the peculiar temporality of the moment of facing death.

In the end, Eddington's facelessness, doubly 'de-faced' by the enlarging effects of the close-up, combines with his skill as an actor to make it possible for us to see him]*as if* for the last time and feel what that truly means. For Eddington becoming unrecognisable is a permanent state of being. But this can also be an everyday phenomenon that occurs in the fleeting time of the changeability of all faces. In both cases, becoming unrecognisable *rehearses* the temporality of the approach of death by bringing into play the sensations associated with the unique awareness of time we experience in that moment. As spectators, we have, I believe, two options: we can either flee from the fullness of death revealed, retreating behind the veils of tragedy and immortality, or, alternatively, we can look directly into the space of facelessness and, in doing so, recognise the other's unrecognisability, their absolute difference from self. To take the latter option, to 'turn back', so to speak, as Orpheus once did, is to enter the space of death and thereby risk our own recognisability. As I attempt to show in the chapters that follow, there are things to be gained by taking this risk, not the least of these being an understanding of visual culture *as* a face of death.

ENDNOTES

i In November 1995, Yitzhak Rabin, then Prime Minister of Israel, was assassinated by an Israeli citizen while leaving a state organised peace rally.

ii A different version of this chapter was published in 1998. See Therese Davis, 'Becoming Unrecognisable', *UTS Review*, 4, no.1 (1998).

iii Maurice Blanchot, *The Gaze of Orpheus and other literary essays*, trans. Lydia Davis (Barrytown, NY: Station Hill, 1981), 100.

iv Arthur Schopenhauer quoted in Zygmunt Bauman, *Mortality, Immortality and Other Life Strategies* (Cambridge: Polity Press, 1992), 13.

v Channel Ten (Australia), *Nightly News*, 9 November, 1995.

vi Wolfgang Kayser, *The Grotesque in Art and Literature*, trans. Ulrich Weisstein (New York: McGraw-Hill, 1966), 16. A good example of this later kind of grotesque imagery is the excessive portraiture of Mannerist painter, Giuseppe Arcimboldo. See Giancarlo Maiorino, *The Portrait of Eccentricity – Arcimboldo and the Mannerist Grotesque* (University Park and London: Pennsylvania State University Press, 1991).

vii Joy Hester, letter to Sunday Read, quoted in Janine Burke, *Joy Hester* (Elwood, Vic: Greenhouse, 1989), 105.

viii Emmanuel Levinas, 'Ethics as First philosophy', *The Levinas Reader*, ed. Sean Hand (Oxford: Basil Blackwell, 1989), 83.

ix Emmanuel Levinas, *Totality and Infinity: An Essay on Exteriority*, trans. Alphonso Lingis (The Hague, Boston and London: Martinus Nijhoff Publishers, 1979).

[x] For a critique of the role of Judaic thought in Levinas' philosophy, see Elizabeth Grosz, 'Judaism and exile: the ethics of otherness', *New Formations*, 12 (1990).

[xi] Also see Michael Taussig, *Defacement: Public Secrecy and the Labor of the Negative* (Stanford, Ca: Stanford University Press, 1999), 245. Here, Taussig associates what he calls 're-facement' with Benjamin's concept of shock effect and waking. He points out that Benjamin borrows this idea of waking or restoring memory lost to consciousness from Marcel Proust and his idea of *mémoire involontaire*.

[xii] Siegfried Kracauer, *Theory of Film: The Redemption of Physical Reality*, intro. Miriam Bratu Hansen (London: Oxford University Press, 1997), 13-18. I am very grateful to Miriam Hansen for drawing this section of Kracauer's text to my attention.

[xiii] Roland Barthes, *Camera Lucida: Reflections on Photography*, trans. Richard Howard (London: Vintage, 1993), 34.

[xiv] Kracauer, *Theory of Film*, 46, 48.

[xv] For a critique of Benjamin's theories of vision, including his idea of the optical unconscious as it relates to film spectatorship, see Miriam Hansen, 'Benjamin, Cinema and Experience: "The Blue Flower in the Land of Technology"', *New German Critique*, 40 (1987): 179-224. Also see Jodi Brooks' chapter 'Between Contemplation and Distraction: Cinema, Obsession and Involuntary Memory' in *Kiss Me Deadly: Feminism and Cinema for the Moment* (Sydney: Power, 1995).

[xvi] Walter Benjamin, 'A Small History of Photography', *One-Way Street and other Writings*, trans. Edmund Jephcott and Kingsley Shorter (London: New Left Books, 1979).

[xvii] See Roland Barthes, *Camera Lucida*, 77. See also Martin Jay, 'The Camera as Memento Mori: Barthes, Metz and the Cashier du Cinéma', in *Downcast Eyes: The Denigration of Vision in Twentieth-Century French Thought* (Berkeley: University of California Press, 1993).

[xviii] Miriam Hansen, '"With Skin and Hair": Kracauer's Theory of Film, Marseille, 1940', *Critical Inquiry*, 19 (1993), 455. See also in that edition of *Critical Inquiry*, Siegfried Kracauer, 'Photography', and trans. Thomas Y. Levin. Levin notes that Kracauer's essay, "Die Photograhie" was first published in the *Frankfurter Zeitung*, 28 October, 1927.

[xix] Hansen, *Skin and Hair*, 447.

[xx] Sarah Webster Goodwin, *Kitsch and Culture: The Dance of Death in Nineteenth-Century Literature and Graphic Arts* (New York: Garland, 1988), 12.

[xxi] Hansen, *With Skin and Hair*, 458.

[xxii] Béla Balázs, *Theory of the Film – Character and Growth of a New Art*, trans. Edith Bone (New York: Dover Publications, 1970), 60.

[xxiii] Sigmund Freud, 'Slips of the Tongue' in *The Psychopathology of Everyday Life*, Vol. 5, trans. Alan Tyson, ed. James Strachey with Angela Richards (Harmondsworth: Penguin, 1985), 94-152. Freud argues that the work of condensation he demonstrated in *Interpretation of Dreams* applies to slips of the tongue. Giving over forty examples and detailed analysis of selected cases, he writes that the aim of this study is to show that 'A similarity of any sort between two elements of the unconscious material – a

similarity between the things themselves or their verbal presentations – is taken as an opportunity for creating a third, which is a composite or compromise idea ... The formation of substitutions and contaminations which occur in slips of the tongue is accordingly a beginning of the work of condensation which we find taking a most vigorous share in the construction of dreams. 100.

[xxiv] See Kracauer, *Theory of Film*, 108. In a section on comedic dialogue, Kracauer observes how speech can be eroded from within. For example, he writes that Groucho Marx's babble serves to 'disrupt the ongoing conversation so radically that no message or opinion voiced reaches its destination. Whatever Groucho is saying disintegrates speech all around him'.

[xxv] For Balázs, the 'invisible face' is a look which *exceeds* expression and discourse. Balázs held the romantic, Platonic view that the face veils a hidden soul and was committed to anthropomorphism: 'When we see the face of things, we do what the ancients did in creating *gods* in man's image and breathing a human soul into them'(60). On Balázs conception of physiognomy, see Gertrude Koch, 'Béla Balázs: The Physiognomy of Things', trans. Miriam Hansen, *New German Critique* 40 (1987): 167-177. See also Maynard Soloman's introduction to 'The Face of Man',*Marxism and Art: Essays Classic and Contemporary* (Sussex: Harvester Press, 1979).

Chapter 2

Reading the Face

Every human face is a hieroglyph which can be deciphered, indeed whose key we bear ready-made within us. —- Arthur Schopenhauer

From the ancients onward, Europeans have puzzled over the face, devising methods for interpreting its secret language. The classical 'science' of physiognomics involves deciphering an individual's nature by comparing his or her physical appearance to certain types of races or animals, the nature of which is supposed to be known. In a treatise on physiognomics attributed to Aristotle, 'physiognomoici' are defined as writers who 'infer a person's idiosyncratic nature from movements, gestures of the body, colour, characteristic facial expression, the growth of the hair, the smoothness of the skin, the voice, conditions of the flesh, the parts of the body and the body as a whole.'[1] This chapter provides a historical overview of physiognomics as a method for reading the face. It also examines the use of physiognomics as a model for interpreting other surface phenomenon by a range of modern 'physiognomoici', including philosophers, such as Schopenhauer, as well as twentieth-century critical theorists, Theodor Adorno and Walter Benjamin.

I: A Mirror of the Soul

References to the face as a mirror of the soul are found in early Greek literature. The face was first conceived as a mirror of the soul by the ancients. The classical science of physiognomics is based on Aristotle's theory of the interdependence of body and soul, an assumption spelt out in the opening lines of a treatise on the topic justifying why there should be such a science:

> Dispositions follow bodily characteristics and are not in themselves unaffected by bodily impulses. This is obvious in the case of drunkenness and illness; for it is evident that dispositions are changed considerably by bodily affections. Conversely, that the body suffers sympathetically with affections of the soul is evident in love, fear, grief and pleasure. But it is especially in the creations of nature that one can see how body and soul interact with each other, so that each is mainly responsible for the other's affections. For no animal has ever existed such that it has the form of one animal and the disposition of another, but the body and soul of the same creature are always such that a given disposition must necessarily follow a given form. Again, in all animals, those who are skilled in each species can diagnose their dispositions from their forms, horsemen with horses, and huntsmen with dogs. Now if this is true (and it is invariably so), there should be a science of physiognomics. (85)

This notion of contiguity between body and soul underlines the use of physiognomics as a diagnostic tool. In the classical age physiognomics was employed to diagnose physical ailments as well as mental illness. These early physiognomic connections between the face and madness later became the basis of twentieth-century practices of clinical psychiatric photography.[ii] As a physiognomist, the diagnostician perceives the face as a symbolic form. This method of interpretation involves analysing the body's so-called 'unchanging traits' as signs of underlying ethical qualities.[iii] Here, the face is regarded as the most telling part of the body. Indeed, the sixteenth-century physiognomist, Giovanni Battista della Porta, claims that the face is representative of the whole: 'the face represents our entire countenance just as it does one's movements, and passions, and moves ...'[iv] However, as della Porta continues, physiognomic analysis can occur only when the face is in a neutral or what he calls 'cool' state: '... it is not unreasonable to be able to judge [the face] at any time, but only when all the soul's emotions and passions have cooled' (90).

But what exactly is the physiognomist looking for in these passionless moments? In addition to its assumption of interdependence between body and soul, the science of physiognomics establishes what Patrizia Magli describes as 'an ethical and passional similarity between all things' (107). In this world view, the nature of particular human types is divined by detecting resemblances between human and other forms, including animals. Take, for example, the following extract from *Physiognomics* in which Aristotle claims to know women (as a special category of souls) based on a zoological physiognomical comparison between female human beings and female animals:

> Now I will try to distinguish first among the animals, what kind of things differentiates them in respect of bravery and cowardice, justice and injustice. The first division which must be made in animals is into two sexes, male and female, attaching to them what is suited to each sex. Of all the animals which we attempt to breed the females are tamer and gentler in disposition than the males, but less powerful, and more susceptible to rearing and handling. This being their character, they have less spirit than males. This is perhaps most obvious from our own case, for when we are overcome by temper, we become less submissive and are more determined in no circumstances to yield to anyone, but we are inclined to violence and to act in any direction to which our temper impels us. But it seems to me that the female sex has a more evil disposition than the male, is more forward and less courageous. Women and the female animals bred by us are evidently so; and all shepherds and hunters admit that they are such as we have already described them in their natural state. ...(I)n each class female has a smaller head, a narrower face and more slender neck than the male, as well as a weaker chest and smaller ribs, and that the loins and thighs are more covered with flesh than in the males, that the female has knock-knees and spindly claves, neater feet and the whole shape of the body built for charm rather than nobility. (109-111)

From a twenty-first-century perspective Aristotle's positivism reveals more about the structural sexism in ancient Greece than the nature of the sexes. But what is of interest, however, is how this zoological method of physiognomics introduces an effect that Magli describes as 'reversed mirrors'. She writes: 'Fixed as emblematic images, animals act as reversed mirrors through which it is possible to recognise the passions, vices and virtues of men. The human world on the other hand ... establishes itself as an interpreting device, and, in turn, imitates a further semiotic process back to animal' (98). For Magli, the use of zoomorphism as a mechanism for analysing human qualities is 'perverse', in the sense that 'it attempts to explain images through other images' (98). Moreover, she argues that animality of this kind constitutes 'a paradoxical situation', for '... if man can recognize himself through comparison to animal, the latter returns man to animality at the very moment in which its form surfaces in a recognizable way on a human face'(100). Magli's notion of reversed mirrors shows how from its origins physiognomics is underlined by a contradictory relation to otherness. As she suggests, the human desire to seek resemblances allows for infinite possibilities of otherness that lead to highly ambiguous forms, such as della Porta's 'character-masks': 'Goat-man, Lion-Man, Bird-Man, Monkey-Man'.[V] At the same time, however, the science of physiognomics is a powerful means of repressing otherness by attributing moral significance to all things and thus limiting meanings produced in the logic of similarity.

II: The Face as Magic Mirror

By the eighteenth century the image of the face as a mirror of the soul had been transformed I such a way that all radical aspects of animality were truly contained. This was due largely to the influence of the Swiss pastor John Casper Lavater's popular *Essays on Physiognomy* (1775-78)[vi] in which the human face is posited as no less than 'a magic mirror' of the face of God:

> GOD CREATED MAN IN HIS OWN IMAGE, IN THE IMAGE OF GOD CREATED HE HIM.
> How exaltedly, how exclusively honourable to man!
> Contemplate his exterior; erect, towering and beauteous – This, though be the shell, is the image of his mind; the veil and agent of that divinity of which he is the representative. How does the present though concealed Deity speak, in his human countenance, with a thousand tongues! How does he reveal himself by an eternal variety of impulse, emotion, and action, as in a magic mirror! Is there not something inconceivably celestial in the eye of man, in the combination of his features, in his elevated *mein*? ... Survey this soul-beaming, this divine countenance; the thoughtful brow, the penetrating eye, the spirit-breathing lips, the deep intelligence of the assembled features! ... What harmony! – A single ray including all possible colours! The picture of the fair immeasurable mind within! (2-3)

For Aristotle, the notion of soul was not restricted to humans: 'The soul, then, is the cause and principle of the living body, and as these are talked of in several ways, so is the soul the cause of the body in the three ways we have distinguished; for it is the cause as that from which the movement itself arises, and as that for whose sake it is, and as the formal substance of ensouled bodies ... (A)ll natural bodies being the soul's instruments, those of plants in just the same way as those of animals, an existing, then, for the sake of the soul' (165-166). In contrast, Lavater's essays betray the author's devout humanism. In an essay on 'lines of animality', Lavater concedes that the body is the animalisation of the soul. But he insists, however, that 'man' is the highest form of God's creatures. As a practice of the image, the face is of interest to Lavater only insofar as it reveals the divine origin of humanity.

There are also other significant differences between Lavater's *Essays* and classical physiognomy, upon which they are modelled. In contrast to Aristotle, who argued strongly for a science of physiognomics, Lavater believed that the idea of making physiognomics into a science was 'folly'. As with the classical and other versions of physiognomics, Lavater's essays insist on a distinction between everyday forms of physiognomical perception, what Lavater calls 'physiognomic sensation', and 'physiognomic interpretation', the latter based on what he claims to be a reliable, comprehensive taxonomy of similarities between temperament and form. His essays also contain a highly regulated set of rules that require the physiognomist to consider not one but all the signs before him. As with his classical predecessors and as a kind of prefiguration of the semiologist, Lavater's method involves the physiognomist considering all the characteristics of the body and face – the size, the shape and individual markings, such as moles and lines. However, unlike his predecessors, Lavater argues that the skill of physiognomic interpretation *cannot* be learnt by all. The reason being that it is, according to Lavater, dependent upon a person having a God-given gift for perception: a special optic power that allows the physiognomist to penetrate the surface wherein he (and in Lavater's thought it was only men) can see all that is good and harmonious. As he writes:

> Physiognomy is a source of the purest, the most exalted sensations: *an additional eye*, wherewith to view the manifold proofs of divine wisdom and goodness in the creation, and, while thus viewing unspeakable harmony and truth, to excite more esoteric love for their adorable Author. Where the dark inattentive sight of the inexperienced perceives nothing, there the practical view of the physiognomist discovers inexhaustible fountains of delight, endearing, moral and spiritual. (43) (my emphasis)

Despite this emphasis on physiognomics benefits to humankind, it seems that many of Lavater's contemporaries were greatly concerned about the potential dangers of this 'additional eye'. In an illuminating essay on the social context and reception of *Essays on Physiognomy*, Michael Shortland reports that there were varied reactions to Lavater's claim to a special optic power. For some, Lavater's additional eye was seen as an eye that could, as Shortland puts it, 'fathom different regions of the body, penetrating to hidden layers of meaning, and prising off deceits and postures' (294). As such, it served as a useful tool in the task of detecting hypocrisy, which, according to Shortland, was at that time a controversial issue. Others, however, responded to Lavater's power to unmask the mysteries of the face by masking up. An entry in the *Encyclopaedia Britannica* (1853-60) on Lavater, as quoted in Shortland's essay, explains that 'Admiration, contempt, resentment and fear were cherished towards the author. The discovery was everywhere flattered or pilloried; and in many places, where the study of human character from the face became an epidemic, the people went masked through the streets' (295). We also know that leading figures in this era expressed concerns about the social impact of physiognomics. In his essays Lavater reports that when he met with Germany's Emperor Joseph II, the emperor queried him extensively about the breadth of potential power in physiognomics. In Lavater's account of the meeting the emperor insists: 'But consider ... should you be able to assign precise principles, and your observations become a certain and attainable science, what a revolution you must produce in the world. All men would view each other with very different eyes' (xxxvii). Convinced that the 'additional eye' upon which the ability for physiognomical interpretation is predicted is a rare, God-given talent, Lavater assured the concerned emperor thus: 'I confess ... that my head frequently turns giddy, only at the thought of all the changes which physiognomy might produce in the mass of the human race – but it will produce no such changes' (xxvii). Lavater's essays demonstrate that he was an imaginative man. But it would seem that the idea of a mechanical device that could make physiognomical perception available to all was beyond the limits of his imagination.

III: Faciality

It is argued that the invention of the camera in the nineteenth century reinvigorated the principles of physiognomy. And how! The camera was crucial to the development and popularisation of influential positivist forms of social categorisation and subjugation, such as Francis Galton's programme of Eugenics and Cesare Lombroso's racist theory of criminality.[vii] Photography's apparent objectivity allowed for it to be easily applied in the service of social forms of surveillance and typification, such as, for example, the introduction of the mugshot as technique in state programmes of law and order and the use of medical photography as a tool for not only diagnosing the ill but also categorising and identifying them for the purpose of state control.[viii] In *Mille Plateau* philosophers Gilles Deleuze and Felix Guattari critique the underlining philosophy of these social and cultural processes, which they refer to as 'faciality'.[ix] Taking a constructivist approach to the face, they argue that 'concrete faces cannot be assumed to come ready-made' (168). Rather, they argue that faces are 'engendered by an *abstract machine of faciality*', which plays a crucial role in processes of signification and what they call 'subjectivisation' (168) – the 'folding process', as Deleuze explains elsewhere, of the interiorization of the outside world in the relation to oneself .[x] As a critique of social and cultural practices of making the face meaningful, faciality is central to Deleuze and Guattari's larger aim of deconstructing formations of power and subjectivity by denaturalizing the body. Their concern in this area is with what the body can do, what it is made to do, and what it incites. This rethinking of the body is largely founded on their reading of Antonin Artaud's image of 'the Body without Organs' (*BwO*): an image in which the head is severed from the body. Unable to serve in its role as prime symbol of the self, the head is, as they say, 'de-facialized'.

There is no doubt that Deleuze and Guattari's critique provides a useful theoretical model for deconstructing formations of power and subjectivity, especially with regard to the use of the face as a technique of individuation. Still, we might want to ask the question of is the face ever only a signifier? Can we rid ourselves entirely of the face?

And would we want to? Starting from these questions, I argue that Deleuze and Guattari's critique of faciality results in an abstracted and obscure image of the face. In their central claim that '*concrete* faces cannot be assumed to come ready-made'(my emphasis) we find a fundamental assumption about the body as some sort of undifferentiated mass that gets worked on by the cultural/social machine of faciality. From the start, the machine-like work of culture is opposed to the unformed mass of the so-called concrete face – a flattened out image comprised of 'white wall, two holes'. For these philosophers, the face is pure appearance. To put it simply, in their world there is no such *thing* as a face. In a longish passage worth considering they argue that if human beings have a destiny it is in fact to be free of the face. That is:

> ... to dismantle the face and facializations, to become imperceptible, to become clandestine, not by returning to animality, nor even by returning to the head, but by quite spiritual and special becomings-animal ... that make *faciality traits* themselves finally elude the organization of the face – freckles dashing toward the horizon, hair carried off by the wind, eyes you traverse instead of seeing yourself in or gazing into in those glum face-to-face encounters between signifying subjectivities. "I no longer look into the eyes of the woman I hold in my arms but I swim through, head and arms and legs, and I see that behind the sockets of the eyes there is a region unexplored, the world of futurity, and here there is no logic whatsoever. My eyes are useless, for they render back only the image of the known ... therefore I close my ears, my eyes, my mouth". BwO. Yes, the face has a great future but only if it is destroyed, dismantled. On the road to asignifying and asubjective (171).

In Deleuze and Guattari's dreamed-up world we are able to pass through the face. The face of the woman has no eyes, only holes through which 'I' (?) might swim and thus, discover some unexplored futurity. From my perspective as a flesh and blood woman, this is the language and the dream of men throughout the ages, here, the colonising dream of discovering hitherto uncharted land attaches to the territory of the body, or, more specifically, the female body. Of course they claim this is not the coloniser's dream. They say that the destruction of the face will not occur through some kind of return to a 'primitive pre-face state': 'We will always be failures at playing Africans or Indians or even Chinese, and no voyage to the South Seas, however arduous, will allow us to cross the wall, to get out of the hole, or lose our face' (188). For Deleuze and Guattari, the aim is to destroy the face, and to do this we need to find ways of 'crossing through it' (189). With some optimism, they conclude that the abstract machine of faciality has two different states: 'The face is absolute deterritorialization; the intersection of significance and subjectivisation. It can also be veritable de-facialization – it frees something ...' (190). As deconstructions of the face, these acts of passing through it take the form of a bi-polar movement between deterritorialization and de-facialization. And in this way, we can see how the abstract machine of faciality may not, as Deleuze and Guattari insists, necessarily resemble the face. But what we can also see in this formulation is that the abstract machine of faciality *operates like a face* in its inherent two-facedness. It would seem that to arrive at the model Deleuze and Guattari propose we do not need to destroy the face. On the contrary, we need only turn to the face itself and its unique dialectical properties.

In an essay on the face and aesthetics George Simmel eloquently reminds us that the human face is never simply a configuration of its parts: eyes, nose, mouth, etc.[xi] As Simmel argues, it is also always an amazing dialectical form that is simultaneously constant and a configuration of endless changes in movements of its parts.[xii] Simmel claims that the dialectic between the constancy and immobility of some parts of the face and the dynamic mobility of other parts constitutes a model of appearances. He supports this claim with reference to the eye. In contrast to Deleuze and Guattari's image of the eyeless woman, Simmel explains that there is no other entity he knows of 'which, staying so absolutely in place, seems to reach beyond it to such an extent; the eye penetrates, it withdraws, it circles a room, it wanders, it reaches as though behind the wanted object and pulls it toward itself' (281). For Simmel, the eye 'epitomizes the achievement of the face in mirroring the soul' (281). And herein lies the truly remarkable contribution of Simmel's critique: he argues that the face achieves the feat of mirroring what is not visible *not* because it provides a window to some reality that Plato insists lies behind appearances, but because it is '... the interpreter of mere appearance, which knows no going back to any pure intellectuality *behind* the appearance' (281). Simmel concludes that in order to understand the unique importance of the face in the fine arts we need to come to an appreciation of the dialectical nature of appearance as 'veiling and unveiling' (281). In other words, we need to recognise the face not simply as a type of image but as a productive model *of* the image.

As I mentioned in the introduction to this book, Michael Taussig makes a similar critical move in his text, *Defacement*, only to take this insight into the face to a new level.[xiii] Taussig reminds us how the Greek word for face is *prosopon* or mask, arguing that in the etymology of the word we find the basis of a deep-seated ambiguity. As a mask or screen, the face is conceived as not only that which can unveil a reality that lies behind it, but also as a means of veiling or concealing truth. Taussig also argues that the 'doubleness' of the face – its function as both mirror and mask – constitutes a secret that Platonic thinking has long sought to conceal. Or as he puts it: 'I take the face to be the figure of *appearance*, the appearance of appearance, the figure of figuration, the ur-appearance, if you will, of secrecy itself as the primordial act of presencing' (3). Taussig uses this conception of the face as a model for his philosophical anthropology of the workings of secrecy in the form of the public secret. He shows how the social forms of what he calls 'defacement' – unmaskings of the mask of the face, or 'defacializations', as he writes in his invocation of Deleuze and Guattari's term – do not expose and thus destroy the secret at stake, but rather serve to reveal the truth of concealment. In this way, Taussig draws upon Deleuze and Guattari's critique while at the same time departs from it by emphasizing the materiality of the face, its inherent doubleness. This a crucial point, for while Deleuze and Guattari's 'crossings of the face' lead to 'unexplored regions', 'a world of futurity', Taussig's philosophy of the public secret shows how physiognomical sensation bought forth in acts of defacement is very much grounded in specific socio-historical experience of the face as a particular practice of the image. In this way, *Defacement* invokes a body of critical theory Taussig refers to as 'radical physiognomics', a tradition of intellectual physiognomy that offers us a way of thinking about the face in terms other than those proposed in Deleuze and Guattari's critique.

IV: Mass Media as Face

In her study of the Weimar period in Sabine, Hake identifies a widespread critical interest in physiognomics: 'in sociological writings on the metropolis (George Simmel), in the morphology of world history (Oswald Spenglar), in the first contributions to emergent film theory (Bela Balasz), in metaphysical speculations on the body (Ludwig Klages, Rudolf Kassner), and in a new theory of temperaments (Kretchner)'.[xiv] Hake speculates that in the destabilizing conditions of modernity physiognomy provided a form of resistance: 'The fear of losing all distinctions of class, gender and race can only be countered with a return to the body as the repository of identity and truth' (118). This notion is evident in Balazs' writings on film. In 1923, he wrote *The Visible Man*, one of the first books on the aesthetics and politics of film, and in which he introduces what would become one of his main themes: the role of the camera in restoring the human image to collective consciousness'.[xv] Writing against what he sees as the detrimental effects of the invention of the printing press, Balazs claims that the film camera 'is at work to turn the attention of men back to visual culture and give them new faces' (284). More than this, he goes on to argue that this new face of man has revolutionary potential, for it constitutes a new visual language, one that can re-educate the senses and thus, unite all of humanity. 'The silent film', he writes 'is free of the isolating walls of language differences. If we look at and understand each other's faces and gestures, we not only understand, we also learn to feel each other's emotions' (288). As a number of critics note, this is basically a romantic notion, indebted less to Marxism than it is to debates in German classical Idealist aesthetics about nature, beauty and expression. Although, as Gertrude Koch points out in her study of Balazs' thinking, 'as Romantic thought', Balazs' film theory 'throws into relief the modernist aspects of Romanticism'.[xvi]

   Not all modern 'physiognomici' were as romantic as Balazs. The writings of Theodor Adorno and Walter Benjamin reveal a much more radical understanding of visual culture as a face. In his 1951 essay 'Cultural Criticism and Society' a reflective Adorno insists that all cultural criticism must become 'social physiognomy': '... the task of criticism must be not so much to search for the particular interest groups to which cultural phenomenon are to be assigned, but rather to decipher the general social tendencies which are expressed in these phenomena and through which the most powerful interests realize themselves. Cultural criticism must become social physiognomy'.[xvii] Adorno first applied the principles of physiognomics in his Radio Research Project, where he analysed the 'voice of radio'. In this group of essays Adorno makes explicit comparisons between the role of the cultural critic and physiognomists: 'A physiognomist tries to establish typical features and expressions of the face not for their own sake but in order to use them as hints for hidden processes behind them, as well as for hints at future behaviour to be expected on the basis of an analysis of the present expression. In just the same way radio physiognomics deals with the expression of the radio voice'.[xviii] Here we see how Adorno's physiognomical theorization of expression differs radically from Balazs' romantic notion. Adorno scrutinizes the features of the voice of radio not then in search of a universal language but rather for the traces of socio-historical totality revealed in these features. In other words, Adorno suggests that the physiognomist, or, in this case, the cultural critic, is crucial, for it is he or she who makes sense of the babble of the sur*face* as it relates to the whole.[xix]

It is important to note that for Adorno the critical act of making sense of the whole is more than an act of academic interpretation. He regarded social physiognomics as a way of undermining the illusion of unity. As a physiognomist, Adorno sees radio as a 'cipher' that continually reproduces the structures of the social reality of the capitalist state. This understanding of surface phenomenon corresponds to Simmel's views in his essay on the aesthetic attraction of the face, mentioned earlier. For Simmel, the significance of the figure of the face in art can be attributed to its 'absolute unity of meaning'.[xx] However, this aspect of the face also makes it vulnerable to the violence of disfigurement. As Simmel writes: 'aesthetically, there is no other part of the body whose wholeness can as easily be destroyed by the disfigurement of only one of its elements. For this is what unity out of and above diversity means: that fate cannot strike at any one part without striking every other part at the same time – as if through the root that binds the whole together' (276). In this way, we could say that Adorno's social physiognomics are an act of disfigurement, for here physiognomic interpretation serves to break the 'spell' of unity formed in the circular pattern of the social.

In *The Origins of Negative Dialectics* Susan Buck-Morss claims that Adorno's familiarity with and choice of physiognomics as a model of analysis was inspired by Walter Benjamin's critical methods, who, she writes, 'had absorbed [physiognomy] from literary-aesthetic rather than scientific channels' (176). There are, however, a number of significant differences between Benjamin's method of intellectual physiognomy and that of Adorno. Adorno's method of social physiognomics is in many ways a straightforward appropriation of the classical principles of physiognomical interpretation, while Benjamin's invocation of physiognomical ways of seeing takes us back to Lavater's distinction between what he calls physiognomic sensation and physiognomic interpretation. As with Lavater and other 'trained' physiognomists, Adorno's social physiognomy emphasizes the role of the interpreting critic. In contrast, Benjamin's emphasizes everyday processes of physiognomic perception and questions of transmissibility, shifting the focus away from the cultural critic toward the spectator. In order to explore the implications of these critical differences I suggest a brief detour through the writings of the German metaphysician, Arthur Schopenhauer, whose interest in physiognomy resonates with Benjamin's critical method.

Reading Schopenhauer's essays we soon discover that he was a devout physiognomist. This is evident in the following extract from one of his essays on history:

> Every human face is a hieroglyph which can be deciphered, indeed whose key we bear ready-made within us. It is even true that a man's face as a rule says more, and more interesting things than his mouth, for it is a compendium of everything his mouth will ever say, in that it is the monogram of all the man's thoughts and aspirations. The mouth ... expresses only the thoughts of a man, while the face expresses a thought of nature: so that everyone is worth looking at, even if everyone is not worth talking to.[xxi]

For Schopenhauer, the 'speech' of the face differs from verbal articulation of conscious thought in that the former provides access to the 'thought of nature'. But what does he mean exactly by nature? In his essay 'On the Antithesis of Thing in Itself and Appearance', Schopenhauer challenges Emmanuel Kant's notion of 'synthetic judgement' in which Kant theorises of the role of the intellect in the processes of perception. Kant claimed that in perception a structure is imposed upon the sense perceptions of the physical world, thus creating a distinction between a 'thing in itself' – that which exists a-priori to perception – and physical appearance. In *The world as will and idea*, Schopenhauer argues that intellect is secondary to will. He also insists that will is not rationality. Nor is will confined to human experience. Rather, Schopenhauer attributes this transcendent will to nonliving matter. Crudely put: will is a kind of inner force of things.[xxii]

It is also important to understand that when Schopenhauer contends that 'the outer reflects the inner' he is not suggesting that the inner truth of things is revealed through a rational imposition of a structure on form. Instead, he puts forth a view that takes us back to the ancients, that is, to be more specific, to the classical physiognomical assumption of contiguity between character and form:

> Because everything in nature is at once *appearance* and *thing in itself* or *natura naturata* and *natura naturans*, it is consequently susceptible of a twofold explanation, a *physical* and a *metaphysical*. The physical explanation is always in terms of cause, the metaphysical in terms of *will*; for that which appears in cognitionless nature as *natural force*, and on a higher level as *life force*, receives in animal and man the name *will*. Strictly speaking, therefore, the degree and tendency of a man's intelligence and the constitution of his moral character could perhaps be traced back to purely *physical* causes. Metaphysically, on the other hand, the same man would have to be explained as the apparitional form of his own, utterly free and primal will. (56) (Original emphasis)

Here, Schopenhauer posits contiguity between will and the physical features of the natural and built environment. But while Schopenhauer is an anti-rationalist, his intention is not to redeem the natural world. Just the opposite. Everywhere Schopenhauer looks he sees only lack and deprivation. His understanding of will is that it is essentially evil and destructive, as manifested in the world's suffering. Or to put this slightly differently, Schopenhauer insists on a pessimistic view of the world in which human existence is basically an experience of suffering. In a short piece titled 'On Aesthetics', for example, he challenges the transcendental notion of the Good found in Socrates' speech on Beauty and the now famous image of 'the wings of the soul', arguing that even here perception of the beautiful is negative, because in aesthetic experience the subject is more conscious than ever of 'the pain and of thousandfold misery' that temporarily subsides in that positive experience (155-156). This is an important point for understanding the significance of physiognomics in Schopenhauer's philosophy of history, where, in one instance, he writes:

> As every man possess a physiognomy by which you can provisionally judge him, so every age also possesses one that is no less characteristic. For the *Zeitgeist* of every age is like a sharp east wind that blows through everything. You can find traces of it in all that is done, thought and written, in music and painting, in the flourishing of this or that art: it leaves its mark on everything and everyone, so that, e.g., an age of phrases without meaning must also be one of the music without melody and form without aim or object. Thus the spirit of an age also bestows on it its outward physiognomy. The ground-bass to this is always played by architecture: its pattern is followed first of all by ornaments, vessels, furniture and utensils of all kinds, and finally even by clothes, together with the manner in which the hair and beard are cut (223).

Just as Schopenhauer believed that any face will inevitably betray human existence as an essential experience of suffering, so too he uses physiognomical theories as a model of the expression of the historical experience of world suffering – 'a sharp east wind' that cuts its way through the surfaces of things leaving a physical trace of the suffering it causes. This powerful negative image of the world as a face, a face violently weathered by the force of the sharp east wind of history, resonates with Benjamin's philosophy of history, although for Benjamin history is *not* an essentialised, universal force, as it is in Schopenhauer's theory of will. As with Schopenhauer, who suggests that architecture bears the impressions of the spirit of the age in its surface detail, Benjamin claimed that the origins of the crisis of experience of modernity can be found in the outmoded, unfashionable Paris Arcades. Fascinated by the Surrealists' fascination with Paris, he observed how in surrealistic experience the city becomes a face, a terrain of surfaces – 'sharp elevations' and 'strongholds'.[xxiii] And in doing so, the surrealist mode of seeing releases what is unconscious.

Benjamin went on to make surrealism the basis of his method of cultural analysis. He extended the surrealistic attitude to the city as a surface to 'overrun and occupy' as a form of revolt against alienation, a way of recuperating what had become alienated and lost to human experience (183), to other cultural phenomenon. For Benjamin, the redeemed image of the past is made visible not through contemplation – not by the application of the 'trained eye' of the cultural critic – but in instances of shock experience. Benjamin's interest in Surrealism as a critical model involved arranging the fragments and debris of the city in such a way that they would blast reality open to reveal the imprint of the history within the city's surfaces in moments of what he calls 'recognizability'. Unlike Adorno's 'critical polemic' of reading cultural forms as images of social truth, or, what he and Simmel perceive as 'the whole', Benjamin's aim was to arrange the fragmentary details of the surfaces of things in such a way that they create a catastrophic juxtaposition. As with the shock of recognition that occurs when a strange face suddenly appears familiar, Benjamin theorizes that the shock experience of surrealistic modes of juxtaposition allow us to recognise what has become estranged to us, the aspects of life from which we have become alienated. The technology of film is central to this method. Benjamin theorized that the camera unleashes an optic power, or more specifically, an 'optic unconscious', to use his term, which blasts open the surfaces of things, releasing the fragments of the past embedded within. Here, the sur*face* is not the embodiment of a transcendental truth. Nor is it a key to a social totality, as Adorno suggests. Rather, in Benjamin's writings the face is a model of how the surfaces of things are penetrable by the 'sharp east winds of history'. For Benjamin the human face, as with all the surfaces of the world, is both *a receptor and potential transmitter* of social and historical knowledge. In this way, Benjamin's choice of physiognomics as a model of cultural analysis allows him to shift the focus away from the interpreting critic toward the viewing subject or spectator. He does this throughout his writings in an elaboration of a materialist aesthetic, a view in which the face of things is conceived as a potential transmitter of social and historical knowledge. The 'trick' as we once referred to this method, involves setting things up in such a way that allows for a shock of recognition to jolt us out of habitual ways of seeing.

ENDNOTES

[i] Aristotle, 'Physiognomics', *Minor Works*, trans. W.S. Hett (London and Cambridge Mass.: William Heinemann Press and Harvard University Press, 1955). 89

[ii] See Hugh W. Diamond, 'On The Application of Photography to the Physiognomic and Mental Phenomena of Insanity', *The Face of Madness: Hugh W. Diamond and the Origin of Psychiatric Photography*, ed. Sander L. Gilman (Secaucus, New Jersey: Citadel Press, 1977).

[iii] Magli, Patrizia. 'The Face and the Soul'. Translated by Ughetta Lubin. In *Fragments for a History of the Human Body, Part Two*. Edited by Michel Feher with Ramona Naddaff and Nadia Tazi, 87-127. New York and Cambridge, Mass.: Zone and MIT Press, 1989. 87-88.

[iv] As quoted in Magli, 90.

[v] See Magli, 'The Face and the Soul', 101-105. On the radical potential of zoomorphic physiognomics, see Michael Taussig's analysis of Sergei Eisenstein's' *The Strike* (1924), where he argues that the mimetic impulse of zoomorphism in twentieth century cultural forms, such as film, unleashes the repressed 'transformative flux' of pre-history that underlines modernity, *Defacement*, 235.

[vi] John Casper Lavater, *Essays on Physiognomy*, 18th edn., trans. Thomas Holcroft, (London: Ward, Lock and Co., n.d.).

[vii] For a discussion of the influence of physiognomics on Galton, see John Gage, 'Photographic Likeness', *Portraiture: Facing the Subject*, ed. Joanna Woodall (Manchester and New York: Manchester University Press, 1997). See also David Green, 'Veins of Resemblance: photography and eugenics', *Photography/Politics II* ed. Patricia Holland, Jo Spence and Simon Watney (London: Comedia and Photography Workshop, 1986). On Lombrosos, see Cesare Lombroso, *Crime, its causes and remedies*, trans. Henry P. Horton (Montclair, New Jersey: Patterson Smith, 1968). For an excellent critique on the

influence of Lombroso's thinking, see Peter Rigby, *African Images: racism and the end of anthropology* (Oxford; Washington DC: Berg, 1996).

viii See John Tagg, *The Burden of Representation: essays on photographies and histories* (Basingstoke: Macmillian, 1988).

ix Gilles Deleuze and Félix Guattari, *A Thousand Plateaus: Capitalism and Schizophrenia*, trans. Brain Massumi (Minneapolis: Minnesota University Press, 1987).

x For an in depth discussion of this concept, see Giles Deleuze, *Foucault*, trans. and ed. Seán Hand (Minneapolis: University of Minnesota Press, 1986). In a chapter titled, 'Foldings, or the Inside of Thought (Subjectivation)', Deleuze engages with Foucault's writings on processes of subjection and the question of interiority in *History of Sexuality*.

xi George Simmel, 'The Aesthetic Significance Of The Face', trans. Lore Ferguson, in *Essays, Philosophy and Aesthetics*, ed. Kurt H. Wolff (New York: Harper Torchbooks, 1959), 277.

xii It should be noted that Deleuze pays considerable attention to this aspect of the face in his cinema book in a chapter on the face and close-up as 'affection image'. He argues that 'the close-up is the face' and describes this affection image, as the 'combination of reflecting, immobile unity and of intensive expressive movements ... constitutes the affect' (87). He goes on to theorise two types of face/images – the thinking face and the feeling face –based on these two aspects of the face – that is, reflective and expressive. Deleuze's insights are of great interest, but overall this is a very different approach to the face as an image to that which is pursued in this book. See Gilles Deleuze, *Cinema 1: The Movement-Image*, trans. Hugh Tomlinson and Barbara Habberjam (Minneapolis: University of Minnesota Press, 1989).

xiii Michael Taussig, *Defacement*,1999.

xiv Sabine Hake, 'Faces of Weimar Germany' in *The Image in Dispute: Art and Cinema in the Age of Photography*, ed. Dudley Andrew (Austin: University of Texas Press, 1997), 118.

xv Reprinted in Maynard Soloman, *Marxism and art; essays classic and contemporary, selected and with historical and critical commentary* (New York: Knopf 1973).

xvi Gertrude Koch, 'Bela Balazs: The Physiognomy of Things' New German Critique, 40 Winter, 1987: 167-178.

xvii Theodor W. Adorno, 'Cultural Criticism and Society', *Prisms*, trans. Samuel Weber and Shierry Weber (London: Neville Spearman, 1967), 30.

xviii Theodor. W Adorno, 'Radio Physiognomik' 1939, trans. by and quoted in Bick Morss, 1977.

xix This aspect of Adorno's thinking is explained by Susan Buck Morss in her discussion Adorno's study of radio in *The Origin of Negative Dialectics* (Hassocks: Harvester Press, 1977). She writes, for Adorno: 'The structure of this totality appeared within the illusionary appearance of the radio voice, but not without the active intervention of the interpreting subject, who unlocked the 'rebus' of surface details, adhering to them with 'exactitude', yet at the same time going beyond them through the mediation of theory to demonstrate that 'the unity' of the radio phenomenon in itself, as far as it really has the structure of a unity, is simply the unity of society which determines all the individual and apparently accidental features – like radio's penetration as a public voice into the private sphere of the bourgeois interieur, its standardizing tendencies despite 'pseudo-individuation', the resulting atomization of radio's mass audience, who passively consumed 'canned' music and whose freedom was limited to switching the station.'(176)

xx. Simmel, 'The Aesthetic Significance Of The Face', 1959, 277.

xxi. Arthur Schopenhauer, *Essays and Aphorisms*, trans. R.J. Hollingdale (Harmondsworth: Penguin, 1970), 232.

xxii. Arthur Schopenhauer, *The world as will and idea*, trans. R. M. Haldane & J. Kemp (London: Routledge & Kegan Paul).

xxiii. Walter Benjamin, 'Surrealism', *Reflections: Essays, Aphorisms, Autobiographical Writings*, ed. Peter Demetz, trans. Edmund Jephcott (New York: Schoken, 1986), 182-183.

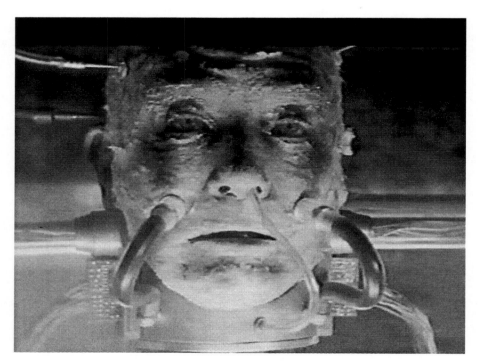

Video enlargement from Cold Lazarus *(Author's collection)*

Chapter 3

Severed Head:

Dennis Potter's Bid For Immortality

The first episode in Dennis Potter's posthumously produced television drama series, *Cold Lazarus*, ends with a startling image: a human head suspended in a large tank of blue liquid nitrogen struggling to open its eyes. In this moment, the newly 'awakened' head confronts a montage of image and sound projected onto a giant liquid screen. From this swirl of colour and form there suddenly emerges a close-up of Daniel Feeld – the dead protagonist from the prequel to this series, *Karaoke*. Here, Feeld, a scriptwriter, is recalling how whenever he was in pain or in fear as a child he would tell himself a story and make believe he was in the middle of a book: 'the one bright, shining thing – '. But before Feeld can complete his sentence the image dissolves into a point-of-view shot: Feeld's friends gathered around his hospital bed, leaning into his face as he gasps for air, as he makes his final request: 'No biographies!' Cutting back to the head in the tank we see that its eyes are now wide open. Suspended between life and death, the head's gaze penetrates the discontinuous images on the screen: stolen memories projected for all to see ...

I: In the Face of Death

When prominent British television journalist Melvyn Bragg heard that his one-time colleague, Dennis Potter, was dying of an incurable form of cancer he approached him with a proposal for a 'final interview'.[1] Bragg's reaction to the news of Potter's death might well be regarded as opportunistic, as he himself considers in his introduction to the published transcript of the interview (ix). However, putting the question of opportunism to one side, Bragg reports that the response to the programme was overwhelming: 'We certainly delivered a television programme which moved and even rocked many of the people watching. Thousands of people reacted directly with phone calls and letters. For some it was a living example of great courage. For others it was an address to the nation in duplicitous and dangerous times. He spoke for sons and their fathers, England and its true traditions, for the present and its infections and yet its possibilities. Of his own work and his last remaining ambition, of the experience of being alive for now' (xiii). In both the interview and the later introduction to the transcript Bragg expresses his great admiration of Potter's courage. He also admits to being overwhelmed by the image of death made visible in Potter's state of physical pain. There are, for example, several occasions during the interview where Bragg hesitates before using the words 'death' and 'dying', while in his introduction he writes: '[t]here was a passion and a translucence before the fact of death and the dreadful pain which moved and impressed so many in a way that could have been achieved by no one else I can think of' (xiii). For Bragg, the visible 'fact' of Potter's death is not representative of some general condition of death and dying. Rather, he attributes this powerful affect to Potter's unique person and manner. He reports that after the taping of the interview one of the crew declared that taping the show had been 'a privilege' (xiii).

Clearly, the award-winning interview 'moved and rocked' both the interviewer and viewers alike. But why exactly? How does this image of a dying man differ from other actual and fictional images of death and dying on television? In production terms the interview is unprecedented. Potter was given privileges television affords to very few others, indeed, levels of treatment reserved for the most distinguished and the most powerful, such as royalty and other heads of state. In recent years the only other comparable event in British television is the BBC's *Panorama* interview with Diana Spencer, the then Princess of Wales. As with the Diana interview, there was minimal editing and little editorial intervention in Bragg's interview with Potter. Bragg writes that his main purpose was 'to give [Potter] as much space and time and energy as possible for as long as possible' (xi). In addition to waving the usual tight controls on time and content, the *Without Walls* interview had a different look from the standard television profile. The interview was taped in a fully visible television studio, with taping beginning as Potter entered the studio and ending only after Potter stood to leave, after he turned to Bragg and said, 'At certain points, I felt I was flying with it ... I'm grateful for the chance. This is my chance to say my last words. So, thanks' (28). Unmasking many of the usually hidden aspects of television, the minimalist production style corresponds to Potter's barefaced presentation of himself as a man close to death, a man with nothing to lose.

The 'naked' style of the interview also serves to expose the relationship between two men who were evidently familiar with one another and more significantly, perhaps, with the medium of television. Reviews of the interview show that some critics were appalled by the evident familiarity of the piece. *Sunday Times*' A.A. Gill, for example, claimed that the event was an indulgent 'in-house eulogy'. He wrote: 'Dotter [sic] represents something very special for a whole generation of television executives, the older producers and editors who still inhabit the top rungs of the big terrestrial franchise holders. They came to television from brilliant universities in the 1960s and 1970s, and they brought a lot of chips and baggage with them'.[ii] It is true that Bragg openly identifies with Potter throughout the interview. In a question about the influence of Potter's working-class origins on his writing, Bragg comments, 'Now, we've both been through that, and we know that things were wrong – awful and terrible and so on – but there's a glow there ... ' (7). In addition to sharing the experience of a British working-class upbringing, Bragg and Potter also shared the route Gill snidely describes as a movement from 'brilliant universities' to television. In defence of the interview, television critic Steve Grant claims that the real 'target' of Gill and others scathing reviews or what he calls 'the backlash against Potter', is the kind of television Potter was associated with – that is, television developed and fostered by people such as Alan Yentob (the then Controller of BBC1) and Michael Grade (the then Chief Executive of Channel Four).[iii] Grant argues that high profile columnists in the

Murdoch-owned press, such as Gill and also A.N. Wilson (*Evening Standard*), despise Yentob and Grade for their egalitarianism and populism, ideals, which, he adds, Potter was committed to throughout his career.

For Potter, British television drama in the nineteen sixties and seventies represented an era of cultural revolution when men – and it was mostly men – like him, like Grade and Yentob, turned to television in the hope of redeeming 'a common culture'. In the interview with Bragg, Potter contrasts this era of 'the kind of broadcasting on television which was such a glory in British life' to today's 'formula-ridden television' (8). It is well documented how throughout his career Potter constructed his commitment to 'common culture' as personal sacrifice. As Bragg writes, 'And I loved the way he (Potter) had poured his talent with apparent recklessness into television. It was a medium which was and still is often thought of as merely ephemeral and just the people's forum' (xii). We would be mistaken, however, to assume that Potter's decision to write for television was simply altruistic or even ideological, as Bragg suggests. Time and again in interviews Potter confessed that his choice to abandon a career in politics and to write for television was motivated by a personal crisis: the need, as he has put it, to 're-create' himself in the crisis of illness:

> My disappointment working on the so-called Labour newspaper, the weirdness of the 1964 election, the crisis of illness, the feeling of failure, the intense despair – all this made me feel blocked and empty. I felt a kind of entropy of the emotions. When I lost the election, I couldn't go back to the *Herald*, which by then had mutated into the pre-Murdoch *Sun*, though in those days it was still a broadsheet paper owned by *The Daily Mirror*. The need to re-create myself coincided with finding the way to do it, which was through drama. I could have gone the 'theatre' way or the 'novel' way, but something – maybe the guilt and anxiety about the gap between my origins and what I had become – steered me toward television. The place of varieties in the corner of the room.[iv]

From this perspective, Gill's dismissal of Potter's work and his characterisation of the success of working-class men is not only snide and childishly put, it also misses the mark. While it is correct to say that Potter's history in television is a crucial element in the shaping of the television event of his death, we also need to recognise that the *Without Walls* interview is entirely in keeping with Potter's history of using television as a way of mediating the effects of the crisis of illness. We could even say that Potter and Bragg use 'the fact' of Potter's dying to do what they each (differently) do best – that is, make television.

For his part, Bragg's decision not to go the usual way such programmes do and use clips from Potter's work resulted in an innovative programme. As I said, the interview looks strikingly different from the standard interview format at that time. The deliberate underproduction, combined with an almost constant focus on Potter's face, created a powerful viewing experience. In Bragg's words: '... for more than 95% of the time we were concentrating on the face of a man facing his own life and death in a way which was to capture the emotions and the admiration of a considerable part of this nation. The simplicity and, if one can risk the word, the nakedness of it gave it luminous power' (x-xi). But while Bragg was rendered silent – indeed, awestruck – by the nakedness of death exposed by the physical pain visible on Potter's face, Potter self-consciously appropriates the powers of death as a means to a quite different end.

Potter's scripts, as well as the many interviews he has given over the years, indicate that Potter conceived himself as an Author in the classic literary tradition. It is not surprising then that this interview also focuses on issues of authorship. In fact, while there are some very moving sections in which Potter reveals his feelings, overall the content of the discussion between Bragg and Potter is remarkably depersonalised. There is little mention of Potter's family, and at no point in the interview does Potter raise the fact that his wife Margaret was also dying of cancer at the time. The only real insight we get into Potter 'the man' is through his thoughts on his experience of dying, thoughts which are, moreover, mediated through his conception of himself as an author. For example, his often cited description of seeing a blossom from his window – the image from which the published transcript takes its title – is a metaphysical image, described by Grant in his review 'as comparable to the imagery of Gerald Manley Hopkins'(22). What we see in this interview for 95% of the time, as Bragg calculates, is not simply the face of a dying man, but rather, the face of a dying author – that is, someone who interprets and represents the experience of facing death in a literary way. This is not to suggest that Potter is somehow false in his presentation of self. My point is simply this: Potter uses the authority of the physical 'fact' of his dying as a way of mediating recognition of himself as an author, in the modern literary sense of the term. The question is, to what end?

In Bragg's view, Potter's imminent death serves to strip back the masks and fictions of the self, revealing an unadorned, pre-cultural self. Throughout the introduction to his interview with Potter Bragg displays the widely held modern understanding of death as a self-concept – that is, death as an event that reveals the hidden self that lies behind the masks of sociality.[v] Everything about this interview, from its naked production style to the line of questioning Bragg pursues, promotes this view of death as a hermeneutic. But Potter himself, I argue, demonstrates a different conception of death and recognition. His demand for recognition in death is, I suggest, a claim to the modern aesthetic point of view of the author immortalised in his work, a point of view in which the personality of the artist, as James Joyce puts it in *A Portrait of the Artist as a Young Man*, 'passes into narration ... finally refines itself out of existence, impersonalises itself, so to speak'. [+]vi[P] And herein lays Potter's dilemma as a 'television author': the modern aesthetic view of the faceless text requires that the text has a life of its own and, as such, it has the potential to outlive the author and hence allow the author's 'voice' to be hard long after he or she is dead. However, television, as we know, is not durable. Just the opposite: it is ephemeral, leaving Potter two options if he wishes to become immortal: he can either seek another 'vehicle' for immortality or he can transform television into something durable. As it turns out, he chose the latter.

Returning to the interview we see that in the final moments of taping Potter seizes his opportunity to become immortal by intervening in television history:

Bragg: *When you knew you were ... you had cancer, you decided to write. One of the things you decided to do was write. What are you writing? We're about a month from when you were told, from 14 February?*

Potter: *... First of all I was on the point of delivery of something that had been commissioned quite a long time ago, called Karaoke, for the BBC...as soon as the news, as soon as I knew I was gonna die, I thought, I can't deliver this, this...whatever I'm doing now is my last work, and I want to be proud...I want it to be, I want it to be fitting. I want it to be a memorial. I want to speak, I want to continue to speak ... (24-25).*

Potter claims he is writing two final television series in order to create a fitting memorial: 'stars in my crown', as he would later claim. But he also wants the series to be more than a commemoration of his creative genius. Rather, as he says, he wants 'to continue to speak'. In this sense, Potter's bid for immortality involves not only having a posthumous existence in the form of his (faceless) writing, but also through the enactment of a form of power that Ross Chambers describes as 'rhetorical presence'[vii]: he seeks the power to continue to speak in a future in which he will no longer physically exist. This takes us beyond the modernist aesthetic point of view of 'voice' toward a more active or interventionist use of fiction. Here, Potter uses the fact of his dying to strike a bargain:

Potter: *What I'd like to see, since it's my last work, and since I have spent my life in television, that life has not been insignificant in television, I would like the BBC's part (Karaoke) to be shown first by the BBC and repeated the same week on Channel 4, and then that inherited audience for the second part, Cold Lazarus, which would have some continuity in terms of character, but could still be ...stand separately, obviously, to be shown first by Channel 4 and repeated by BBC (27).*

Potter's 'last request' regarding the production of his two final television drama series transforms an otherwise interesting program into a television event. In the days immediately following the UK broadcast, BBC 1 and Channel 4 announced that they would grant Potter his dying wish, undertaking to co-produce what turned out to be the most complex and expensive co-production in the history of British television drama to date. This willingness on the part of the heads of otherwise competing British television corporations is a clear indication of Potter's unique status as a television author. But more than this, perhaps, it is a telling reminder of how becoming immortal requires more than simply excelling in a given field of social or cultural life. As Zygmunt Bauman argues in his study of immortality in the media age, it also involves being recognised as such by the living. In other words, the power to grant immortality lies with the living not the dead, a fact that Potter seems to have been very much aware of.[viii]

II: The Mask of Writing

I do not believe what writers say about themselves, except when they think they are
not saying it about themselves. This is not necessarily because they have less probity than

others ... but because the masking of the Self is an essential part of the trade. Even, or especially, when 'using' the circumstances, pleasures and dilemmas of one's own life—
Dennis Potter

Karaoke, the first of Potter's two posthumously produced drama series reflects a number of interesting issues of recognition that arise in the event of Potter's death. In his book length study of Potter's writing John Cook suggests that *Karaoke* is the piece in which 'the "Author" will have demonstrably made the "nearest" approach to himself'.[ix] It is easy to see why Cook would take this view. A thriller, *Karaoke* tells the story of the last week in a scriptwriter's life and revolves around his discovery that the plot of his latest film script is unfolding around him in the events of his everyday life. While the film's production team try to minimise the damage caused by these 'coincidences', including the discovery of a real-life replicate of the villain in the film, the writer struggles with the concept of predestination and his imminent death from cancer. Clearly, *Karaoke* is uncannily similar to Potter's situation. Still, we might ask if this self-referentiality constitutes an unmasking of the self? After all, behind which mask do we find the face of Potter?: Feeld the writer; Balmer the fictional director; the leading actor in Feeld's film, played by actor Ian Diarmind, who bears an uncanny resemblance to Potter; or what about the aged face of a Muslim woman who appears intermittently throughout the series as a 'deaths-head' figure, and who, in one scene repeatedly shouts out that she is aged sixty-one – the same age as Potter. In the end, any attempt to discover the 'real' Potter in the ever-changing masks of *Karaoke* is futile, for as with other scripts written by Potter *Karaoke* is designed to be elusive. Or as W. Stephen Gilbert suggests in his biography of Potter, the art of masking is central to Potter's work: 'The masks are slipped on so expertly – or is it unconsciously? – that you lose track of where the latest transformation occurred ... so the assumption of masks, the playing of games with the reader, viewer or interviewer becomes a prevailing method. It is a process of concealment by seeming revelation. He eludes as he illudes as he alludes'.[x]

So if it is not Potter 'the man' behind the mask of writing, then what else might lie behind these final words? To answer this we need to look at Potter's unique status as a television author and examine how this reputation was in large part mediated through his relation to the viewing audience. As we saw in the earlier section of this chapter, Potter has a reputation of using television as a way of redeeming common culture. From the beginning of his career as a television writer Potter also had a special status in television culture as an author. These two forms of recognition are not unrelated. In 1987, Rosalind Coward responded to the then recent season of Potter plays and films on British television by raising the question of television authorship. Analysing the publicity and reception of the event, she argued that 'we can witness the simultaneous 'literary' commitment to the idea of an individual author, and the desire to elevate the status of television through the existence of 'great' television writers'.[xi] For Coward, the desire on the part of those within and outside of television to use authorship as a way of raising the status of television to that of art, limits our understanding of the specificity of television and of what individual programmes can contribute to that understanding. A case in point for Coward is the reception of Potter's drama series, *The Singing Detective*, first broadcast on BBC television in the UK in 1986. She argues that 'far from "authorship" being necessary to guarantee significance, the concept, if anything, seems to get in the way, and block recognition of some of the truly radical aspects of the series'(84). For Coward, the most significant thing about this series is that it can be seen to 'emphatically reveal the importance of the viewer as the place where the meaning of the text ultimately (if anywhere) resides' (86).

Despite Coward's convincing arguments, popular criticism of Potter's work continues to focus on the question of authorship. One of the first book-length critical study's of Potter's work also takes this view, forcefully contesting Coward's critique of the problematic construction of Potter as a television author. A proponent of auteurism, Cook's text focuses on textual and production processes. He makes the argument that the system in which Potter worked 'implicitly encouraged the writer to think of him or herself as self-expressive artist' (7). He writes: 'In contrast to Coward's critiques ... individual thematic and stylistic continuities can be shown to exist and are readable across the range and variety of Potter's writing for the medium' (7). Guided by Potter's own assessment of his work, Cook's thesis is that the origin of Potter's work lies in his affliction. He argues that Potter's physical crisis was primarily a spiritual crisis and traces the significance of this in Potter's work. He claims that this crisis can be traced back to Potter's early work, such as *Brimstone and Treacle*, where despair in illness takes the form of a preoccupation with Old Testament notions of 'The Fall'. He also claims that Potter's first novel *Hide and Seek* marks a major shift in Potter's spiritual development. Cook suggests that this self-reflexive, self-conscious novel – about a man who believes someone is writing about him, an author who admits to manipulating a character, and so on – is a model of the spiritual movement toward 'hope' that continues in Potter's later diverse writings (302): 'Disease took [Potter] out of the real world of politics and current affairs (a world with which ... he had already become disillusioned) and made him more concerned with the inner life of the individual and ultimately, with spiritual questions about the nature of personal suffering, death and God' (19). Echoing a sentiment we often hear in the age of 'the good death', Cook argues that although 'terrible in its physical nature, Potter's disease performed a useful function for him. Issues of politics and social class which had pre-occupied him as a young man paled into insignificance beside the need to survive and to look into himself in his attempt not only to cope emotionally with the fact of illness but by so doing possibly to find a cure' (19-20). Cook's Neo-romantic view severs the politico-social aspects in Potter's work from the artistic/creative aspects by claiming that Potter's relation to language was mediated by a religious sensibility generated by the crisis of illness. In other words, writing is constituted as Potter's 'cure' and his salvation.

While I do not agree with Cook's thesis, I can agree that it is difficult to avoid the figure of the author in Potter's writing, including the many commentaries Potter has made on his own work. As Coward has suggested, however, Potter's construction of himself as author and the part that this construction has played in the reception of his work, cannot be overstated. Moreover, Potter's self-conscious construction of himself as author relates precisely to the aspects of Potter's writing that Cook seeks to suppress: that is, the social and political dimensions of the work. In the most recent book-length study of Potter, Glen Creeber observes how, '[i]t is surprising that a man who consistently referred to himself as 'reclusive by nature' feels the need to give so many interviews, often going over profoundly personal details and facing the same biographical questioning'.[xii] Creeber also makes the important point that by the end of his life, Potter had very much become a celebrity, 'giving interviews not only to British "art programmes" like *Omnibus*, *Arena* and *The South Bank Show*, but chat shows like *Whicker!* And *Wogan*'(13). In fact, in the later years of his life Potter's notoriety came to overshadow public reception of him as an author. In response Potter used numerous public occasions, such as talk shows, to defend the sovereignty of the imagination.

Looking at *Karaoke* from this perspective, the series is not so much an unmasking of the 'real' Potter but a use of the mask of writing as a final, public demand for recognition of the sovereignty of the author in the age of celebrity and notoriety. As the plot of *Karaoke* unfolds, we discover that Feeld is dying. We also see a number of coincidences emerge that lead Feeld to believe that his script is shaping real-life events. He discovers that there is a 'real-life' thug called Pig Mailion, who, like the villain in the film, runs a karaoke club in the East End area of London. There is also a hostess called Sandra, who works at Mailion's club. And again, there is 'real-life' blackmail and duplicity occurring in the cutting-room. In a self-conscious reference to Potter's own life, it turns out that Balmer, the fictional director, is engaged in an obsessive, extramarital affair with the lead actress from the film who, unbeknown to him, is connected to Mailion and is planning to blackmail him. This complication in the already weighed-down plot is a thinly disguised reference to the scandal of Potter's *Blackeyes*, a series that marked the beginning of Potter's notoriety. The rumours that surrounded the production of that series made Potter a familiar face on the pages of UK tabloids, branding him with the tag, 'Dirty Den', while the series itself added further fuel to the fire. Critics at the time generally agreed that the work was sexist, gratuitous and indulgent.

As I suggested above, in response, Potter took every opportunity he possibly could to defend what he called the sovereignty of the imagination and, by implication, his reputation. When Potter was invited to give the James McTaggert memorial lecture at the Edinburgh International Television Festival in 1993, he struck out at television executives and viewing audiences alike. He argued that there was no longer a place for his style of quality critical television. He blamed free-market privatisation for the 'dumbing down' of television viewers, claiming they have become dulled by formulaic television. 'The turned off TV set', he said, 'picks up a direct or true reflection of viewers, subdued into a glimmer on its dull, grey tube'.[xiii] But notoriety is a vicious circle: the more Potter protested against the tabloidisation of television, the more his reputation as an author of the capital A type faded in contrast to his increasing notoriety. In *Karaoke* the figure of the author is much more contrite than Potter himself, actively seeking forgiveness and understanding for his powerlessness in the face of desire.

This reading of *Karaoke* as an attempt by Potter to reassert his status as author over and above his notoriety is amplified in the protagonist's profound change of heart about the role of the writer. Coward once argued that Potter's work was committed to giving semantic power to the viewer. Such faith is questioned throughout *Karaoke*. In the first two episodes Feeld is preoccupied with controlling the effects of his writing. Two thirds of the way through the series a major shift occurs: Feeld learns that he did not in fact invent the characters in his film but rather the coincidences that have led him to believe that his words 'are out there', as he puts it, constitute a phenomenon called 'cryptonesia'. It turns out that the story he had written is based on a newspaper report he once read and had long since forgotten. In the face of this discovery, the author confronts his impotence. Hence, when his evasive doctor suggests to him that he should put his affairs in order and does anything that he has specially wanted to do, Feeld's responds with a word-play in which writing and life converge as one and the same thing:

Feeld: *Well I was about to write a screenplay about virtual reality and cryogenics, a frozen head, you know, and medical student types, I suppose...*
Doctor: *And how long does it take you this scribble, scribble, scribble?*
Feeld: *About 12 weeks and a bit. I usually reckon on 88 days. Any chance of putting the final full stop in place. I mean there's not all that much point in say getting two thirds of the way through. I don't get paid by the word or per page – More's the pity!*
Doctor: *I couldn't guarantee that you would be able to finish.*

At this point in the series, there is drawn-out silence, during which time a close-up reveals a look that crosses Feeld's face like some kind of seismic change of heart. Feeld finally replies that he will have to make the screenplay 'a bit shorter, with a nice, easy plot'. And the word game resumes:

Feeld: *There's an old favourite, for example, about who it is you would kill and help out humanity if you had say, eight and a bit weeks more or less to go.*
Doctor: *Yes – I've often wondered who I would execute if in such a circumstance. Apart from the secretary of State Health, of course.*
Feeld: *Of Course!*
Doctor: *Yes, I would say that such a plot was about right.*

Recapping the plot of *Karaoke*, Feeld tells the doctor that when he was in pain he went 'kinda dippy'. He says that he thought a play he had written had 'somehow gotten out into the world like a contagious disease – my words, my script, wandering about out there in front of me'. As we know from his interviews, the idea of words having a life of their own, existing in some 'bracketed-off' space, was crucial to Potter's survival of his illness, indeed, one of the main ways in which he managed the excruciating pain of arthropathy. Here, the scriptwriter is forced to face the fact that his words cannot change the world. He admits to the doctor that he now realises 'there's been another story going on all the time'. As Feeld explains:

I always used to tell myself a story when I was in fear as a child and believe I was in the middle of this kind of book, the one, bright book, which was the shape of meaning... I can tidy up all the bits and bobs, find the shape ... I'm back in charge of my own story. I can take control now. I've got it back in my own hands. I know what to do now.

For Feeld, knowing what to do involves asserting his authority in an attempt to regain semantic control. In the final scene of the series, Feeld, having tidied up his affairs, as they say, makes his way to the East End karaoke club where the story began. In a final gesture of self-reference, beautifully realised by Renny Rye's direction and Albert Finney's performance, the writer lip-syncs the melancholic tune, 'Pennies from Heaven' before turning to shoot the villain Pig Mailion. In terms of the plot, Feeld's violent act of killing, or, in his doctor's words, 'execution', redeems the author. Indeed his decision to kill the 'real-life' villain is a heroic rescue of the story's working-class victim. The ending can also be read as an allegory of Potter's re-conception of the relationship between the television author and the viewer. In *Karaoke*'s only love scene Feeld tells Sandra that all of her troubles will soon be over because in the event of his imminent death he has arranged for her and her mother to be generously provided for. However, there is a catch. Sandra must promise to behave as he insists she should. 'I promise, I bloody promise', she cries, in her best cockney accent. Convinced by her apparent sincerity, Feeld tells this young, attractive, working-class woman who has, in the span of a week, become the love of his life, that he has written down 'in a clear way, in a language that you will understand', what she is to do when he is no longer around to protect her. He then asks her to seal the deal with a kiss. But having kissed him, Sandra quickly turns on her heels and tells the writer she intends to carry out her plan to kill the villain. What Sandra doesn't know, however, is that Feeld predicted that she could not be trusted to accept the ending he arranged and thus he had taken the necessary precaution of stealing her gun. With the loaded gun now in his hands, the author makes his way to the karaoke club, and, as I mentioned earlier, sings one final tune before proceeding to execute the villain with a single shot to the head. If this ending is, as Cook and others suggest, an unmasking of Potter, then what we see here is, surely, Potter's desire to redeem himself as the saviour in/of the plot, an image of the writer as an all-powerful form of social conscience, in this case, saviour of the working-class television viewer who in the eyes of this author cannot be trusted with semantic control.

IV: Death's Head

In *Karaoke*, the author, who stands in for Potter's authority, commits textual suicide in the name of the sovereignty of the imagination. The problem is that this suicidal rescue of the blinded viewer leaves Potter without a voice and thus unable to dictate the terms of his recognition in death. This apparent voicelessness is, I suggest, the reason behind the sequel – *Cold Lazarus*. In this second series, Potter turns for the first time in his career to science fiction, and the result is fresh and innovative. The story of *Cold Lazarus* takes place some three hundred and seventy-four years in the future and is set in and around a pharmaceutical laboratory where the cryogenically frozen head of the dead writer from the former series is the object of scientific experiments in memory retrieval. The series opens with the announcement of a breakthrough in the research process – a team of researchers watch in awe as the first transmissions of the head's visual and aural memories are projected onto a giant liquid screen. Responding to the 'wonder' of the sight of a retrieved grab of a football final from 1974, the head of the research unit tells her team that these fragments offer them access to 'an authentic past', and even perhaps 'an escape'. This begs the question of an escape from what? It turns out that the 'Lazarus Operation', as the memory-retrieval project is known, takes place in a future where existence is entirely mediated. A thinly disguised allegory of a future world wholly dominated by private entertainment enterprises, *Cold Lazarus* is Potter's final statement on television culture.

We quickly learn that life in the future is an Orwellian nightmare in which every aspect of daily life is under surveillance. This is not a totalitarian state, for as we learn there are two competing forces. First there is the pharmaceuticals consortium that funds the 'Cold Lazarus' project. It's controlled by the overbearing, oversexed, penny-pinching Martina Masden. Her rival is David Siltz, who is clearly modelled on the real-life television and print mogul, Rupert Murdoch. In true science fiction tradition, we also learn that there are plans afoot for a social revolution and that the Lazarus Operation is about to become the site of a struggle for the future of this fantasy media world. The struggle involves a number of players. First, there are the two media moguls who both see the head's value only in terms of capital gain. Then there is the group of scientists who, like the hermeneutic critics Potter so despised throughout his life, try to access the authentic experience that they believe resides in the head's memories in the name of knowledge. Completely powerless in its suspended state, the fate of the head rests with the revolutionary group *RON* (Reality or Nothing). They plan to rescue the head from invasions of any kind. For RON, the head must be protected at all costs, for it is the sacred site of consciousness and human spirit.

The idea of the head as the site of consciousness and imagination, as the primary site of individuation, underlines the practice of cryonics – the preserving of either the whole body or just the heads of the newly dead for the purpose of future revival. The cryonic process of freezing heads in liquid nitrogen was first developed by US scientist Robert Ettinger.[xiv] Ettinger was reportedly inspired by a 1930s work of science fiction titled *The Jameson Satellite* – a story about a scientist who orbits the earth in a sealed satellite for many years only to be later rescued and revived by aliens. By adapting this model of life suspended in outer space for a conception of life after death, cryonics posits the space of death as a suspension of time. For cryobiologists and their supporters, who are mainly future 'patients', or 'cryonaughts', as they call themselves, being frozen is a means of avoiding the finality of death. One cryobiologist and well-known science fiction writer, Gregory Benford, describes cryogenics as a process similar to sleep. He believes that in some future time we will be able to 're-boot' frozen/sleeping consciousness in the way consciousness is, to use his term, re-booted every morning when we wake. In this metaphor, time is suspended in death in the same way that we become unaware of time while sleeping. But perhaps the most interesting thing about the cryogenic view of the head is the fact that cryobiologists suggest that a 're-booted' consciousness will know itself in some future time. That is to say, not only is time suspended in the freezing process, but this process is also a means of preserving self-consciousness. In the *Quantum* special, Benford explains that in cryonics the 'patient' – 'Let's call him Fred', he says – 'goes to sleep as Fred and wakes up [meaning he is revived] as Fred'. Despite this vision of the future being a new-world in which anything is possible, including cheating death, the technologies of immortality are very much grounded in a transcendental philosophy of the self.

In *Cold Lazarus*, the question of self-sameness in death is raised in several ways. In the final scenes of the series, members of *RON* sacrifice their lives to protect the head/the writer/Potter from further invasion and memory theft. Herein lies the symmetry of the two series: in *Karaoke*, the writer sacrifices his life for the sake of the sovereignty of the imagination. Here, the viewer is invited to identify with the revolutionaries and in doing so sacrifice his or her 'life' for that sovereignty. The head's desire to be free of critical and personal 'invasion' is finally achieved in the series spectacular ending. Rescued by RON and unplugged, the head spills forth its final images. Using special digital effects that cost in the vicinity of £400,000[xv], this image of death as a release from critical invasion takes the form of a montage of fragments from the writer's memory: scenes from Potter's many drama series, spectacular images from early cinema, as well as other fragments from popular culture, including televised football finals. The sweep of colour culminates predictably in a final wash of white light that serves to signal the end of the tunnel of the passage from life to death. Over a symphony of soundtracks from Potter's series and the loud cheers of a football final crowd, the writer embraces death by letting out a loud, resounding, Joycean 'Yes!'

But of course this is not the end. As I have suggested throughout this book, the face has an extraordinary capacity to turn on itself. Here, despite all Potter's greatest efforts to ensure control over the semantic meaning of his final piece of work, the ending is, like all endings, deferred. In this case, the fantastic image of the severed head that Potter invented as a lesson in the sovereignty of the imagination turns on its author to allow for a very different view on authorship than that which its author intended. But then, according to Walter Benjamin, this is the nature of allegorical objects. In *The Origin of German Tragic Drama*, Benjamin argues that allegory is more than an aesthetic form or symbol.[xvi] It is not 'a mere mode of designation' (162), 'a playful illustrative technique'(162). In his analysis of the work of German allegorical poets, he shows that allegory is 'a form of expression, just as speech is expression, and, indeed, just as writing is' (162). This is most clearly seen in the allegorical poets' use of the skull or 'death's head' as an emblem of history. Benjamin writes:

> Everything about history that, from the very beginning, has been untimely, sorrowful, unsuccessful, is expressed in a face – or rather in a death's head. And although such a thing lacks all 'symbolic' freedom of expression, all classical proportion, all humanity – nevertheless, this is the form in which man's subjection to nature is most obvious and it significantly gives rise not only to the enigmatic question of the nature of human existence as such, but also of the biographical historicity of the individual. This is the heart of the allegorical way of seeing, of the baroque, secular explanation of history as the

Passion of the world; its importance resides solely in the stations of its decline. The greater the significance, the greater the subjection to death, because death digs most deeply the jagged line of demarcation between physical nature and significance (166).

For Benjamin, the baroque emblem of the death's head is a dialectical image. It can be read as the mortification of human life, but it is also an image of 'nature in decay' – nature's subjection to the power of death. To see allegorically, he argues, is to see the imprint of history, to see how history survives in the world of dead or discarded things. The allegorical object does not therefore signify (designate), but it *reveals* in its two-facedness the processes of signification. Benjamin writes: 'In the field of allegorical intuition the image is a fragment, a rune. Its beauty as a symbol evaporates when the light of divine learning falls upon it. The false appearance of totality is extinguished. For the *eidos* disappears, the simile ceases to exist, and the cosmos it contained shrivels up. The dry rebuses which remain contain an insight which is still available to the confused investigator' (176).

Here, allegorical insight reveals the specific nature of televisual processes of signification. When Potter's severed head releases its supposedly secreted memories of a past life, as it makes its passage from the world of the living to that of the dead, it is emptied of any sense of self. The head is de-faced. Or to use Benjamin's term, it becomes a 'death's head', a 'fossil' of a past life. But as Benjamin argues, it is in the precise moment of being emptied of signification that the hollowed-out death's head opens up the allegorical way of seeing. From this perspective, Potter's severed head turns on itself to reveal its own history of signifying. The story invites us to see the images that pour forth from the head as references to a reality that lies behind the fiction, namely, references to Potter the man – evidence of 'a glorious past in television history', as Potter once said, an era in which Potter reigned as television's one and only author. But what is revealed in this montage of memories is the history of this kind of signifying. As discontinuous fragments, the images released by the head in the throws of death do not so much represent an era of television and cinema, but rather, they embody the modern experience of mediated existence: grabs from televised football finals, memorable key images from Potter's drama series, such as *Pennies from Heaven* and *The Singing Detective*, the unforgettable spectacle of carnival and early cinema. Seen as images of television culture these discarded fragments are not some kind of representative sample of a pre-Murdoch authentic past in television. On the contrary, they are images of the history of television in the present: we see in the most obvious way that television itself is very much the data of both individual and collective memory. We can also see that this is a different conception of history from the notion of tradition that Potter uses in his bid for immortality.

The television event of Dennis Potter's death, including the two final, posthumous drama series, helped to secure a place for Potter in the annals of television history. But at what cost? If anything, we might say that the events resulted in what Bauman calls 'the destruction of immortality'. And, as Bauman argues: 'With its arch enemy, immortality, safely out of the way – in the geriatric ward, if not yet in the coffin – mortality creeps back uninvited. Its face blinks in each ephemeral moment which promises more than it can deliver and vanishes before it can be taken to court. One cannot erase this face. One can only blot it out with a thick coat of lurid paint' (199). It is generally agreed by critics, including Potter's most loyal fan, Steve Grant, that Potter's two final interconnected series were not 'stars' in Potter's crown, as Potter had once hoped they would be. Rather, they turned out to be a spectacular event 'for the duration'. Potter's extravagant wish to see a co-production between rival channels ended disastrously. As McNulty argues, the combination of low ratings and the many problems involved in co-production mean that we are unlikely to see a project of this kind again. Further, by staging the event as he did, including, as I have argued, exploiting the fact of his dying, Potter added to his notoriety. On the recent occasion of Potter's birthday, BBC radio's tribute to him, listed his 'great' works. For the most part, however, the segment focussed on the event of his death and his 'memorable performance' in the interview with Melvyn Bragg: the face of an author is, here, displaced by the ghoulish face of death.

As I have argued throughout this chapter it is precisely these places where the face of death is made visible redeems Potter's work by bringing us closest to 'the real stuff' of Potter's contribution to television. Dennis Potter wanted to be recognised as a saviour of the working class; he hoped his 'quality' television would release working-class viewers from the chains of class imprisonment in Great Britain, just as education had once served to release him. He did this by writing the story of his liberation over and over through a myriad of different masks, all the while trying to keep in question the 'true' face of Dennis Potter. In the final series it becomes obvious that the face Potter spent his life concealing behind the mask of writing was in fact a faceless 'death's head'. Yet, as I argued, in the end, it is this death's head, this relic of television that provides us with a truly memorable image of the significance of television in modern life. In the snatches of television culture that spill forth from the severed head we can recognise not now the face of a great television author but something of the unique temporal properties of television. As an image of fragmentation and transitoriness, Potter's simulated death is a vivid display of the role television plays in the structuring of contemporary experience, which is, I suggest, precisely what the best of Potter's scripts enable us to see.

ENDNOTES

[i] Dennis Potter, *Seeing the Blossom – Two Interviews and a Lecture* (London and Boston: Faber and Faber, 1994).

[ii] A. A. Gill, 'Overindulged to the bitter end', *The Sunday Times* (UK), 28 April, 1996, C12.

[iii] On the backlash against Potter in the British press see Steve Grant, 'Dead man talking', *Time Out*, 1339 (April 17-23 1996): 22-24; 'Manifesto', *Time Out* 1342 (May 8-15, 1996): 13.

[iv] Graham Fuller ed., *Potter on Potter* (London/Boston: Faber and Faber, 1993), 14.

[v] For an overview of this attitude, see Peter Kostenbaum, *Is Their an Answer to Death?* (Englewood Cliffs: Prentice Hall, 1976), 7.

[vi] James Joyce, *A Portrait of the Artist as a Young Man*, ed. Hans Walter Gabler with Walter Hettche (New York and London: Garland, 1993), 242.

[vii] Ross Chambers, 'Visitations: Operatic Quotation in Three AIDS Films', *UTS Review* 2, no.2 (1996), 55.

[viii] See Zygmunt Bauman, *Mortality, Immortality and Other Life Strategies* (Cambridge: Polity Press, 1992).

[ix] See John Cook, *Dennis Potter: A Life on Screen* (Manchester: Manchester University Press, 1995). See also, Steve Grant, 'Facing the music: Potter's swansong probes a writer's life', *Time-Out*, 1340 (24 April – 1 May, 1996): 165.

[x] W. Stephen Gilbert, *'Fight and Kick and Bite' – The Life and Work of Dennis Potter* (London: Hodder and Stoughton, 1995), 28.

[xi] Rosalind Coward, 'Dennis Potter and the question of the television author', *Critical Quarterly* 24, no.4 (1987), 79.

[xii] Glen Creeber, *Dennis Potter Between Worlds: A Critical Reassessment* (Houndsmill, Basington, Hampshire and London: Macmillan Press, 1998), 13.

[xiii] Potter's lecture is republished in Potter, *Seeing the Blossom*, 52.

[xiv] Quantum, ABC (Australia) 23 June, 1996. For more information of cryonics, including Ettinger's 'pioneering' text, *Prospect of Immortality* see the American Cryonics Society's web pages: wysiwyg://23http://www.jps.net/cryonics/ (last updated 14/09/99). For a succinct overview of cryonics in North America, see Roy Rivenburg, 'The Iceman Goeth', *Los Angeles Times*, 'View', (2 March, 1994),1 and 6.

[xv] For details of the budget and other aspects of the production of the two series see Mark McNulty, 'Last Testament' *Broadcast*, 8 March, 1996, S12-13.

[xvi] Walter Benjamin, *The Origin of German Tragic Drama*, trans. John Osborne, intro. George Steiner (London and New York: Verso, 1977).

Video enlargement from Mabo: Life of an Island Man *(Author's collection)*

Chapter 4

'Mabo': Name Without a Face

For readers outside of Australia the name 'Mabo' probably means very little, if anything at all. In Australia, however, 'Mabo' is a household word. It is an abbreviation for *Mabo and others v. The State of Queensland (No2) (1992)*[i]: the landmark legal case in which the High Court recognise d indigenous people's ownership of land prior to British occupation thus overturning the nation's founding myth of *terra nullius* ('an empty land'). Since this judgement, the word 'Mabo' has come to stand for the whole issue of indigenous land rights and native title legislation. As Jeremy Beckett, anthropologist and witness for the plaintiffs, writes in his commentary on the decision, 'media and politicians have added a new word to the Australian vernacular ... if it has not already become a verb, it soon will'.[ii] For Beckett, the overuse of 'Mabo' in popular discourses has resulted in a number of disastrous effects, including the overshadowing of the fate of the leading litigant, Eddie Mabo, who spent more than 10 years of his life fighting for recognition of his and other indigenous peoples' land rights. (7). To put it simply, 'Mabo' is *a name without a face*. In this chapter I examine this cultural oversight, this gap between a judgement and a historical subject in a close analysis of *Mabo – Life of an Island Man* (1997) – an international, award-winning film that commemorates Eddie Mabo's life and his achievements.[iii] Drawing on several different conceptions of defacement, I show how this film presents events following the High Court decision as a *de-facement* of the name, and how its attempt to compensate for this injustice by *giving the name a face* inadvertently reproduces the particular violence of defacement. I also show how this textual defacement opens up a space for a second, more radical perspective on the relationship between the name and the face.

I: Film as Prosopopoeia

When *Mabo – Life of an Island Man* was first screened at the 1997 Sydney International Film Festival, it received a standing ovation that lasted more than five minutes and was voted Best Documentary Film. Since then, it has won numerous other national and international film awards.[iv] It has also had a successful national theatrical release and has been screened on national television (ABC) in prime time on several occasions. Reviews indicate that this positive reception is largely due to the distinctive personal style of the film.[v] John Ryan, for example, writes: 'Moving away from his earlier treatment of Mabo-the-case, Graham's film has brought Mabo-the-Man much closer to us'.[vi] The film uses first person narration, recounting throughout details about the making of the film and the relationship between the film-maker and its subject. It also uses testimonies by family members and friends, as well as several dramatisations of events in Mabo's life and other intimate knowledge, such as the actor Bob Masa's astounding reading of Mabo's love letters to his wife, Bonita.

A number of reviews and feature articles suggest this intimate style of film-making brings us closer to the significance of the historic judgement than a more conventional documentary could. Tom Ryan encapsulates this view in his description of the film as 'an intimate history'.[vii] These sentiments are reiterated in the introduction to the published screenplay of the film where Graham writes: 'The success of the film in Australia indicates that there is a willingness amongst Australians to embrace reconciliation and social justice, *provided* the issue can be made to touch them personally'.[viii] (Emphasis added) The intimate proximity of face-to faceness is achieved by the deployment of several techniques in what Deleuze and Guattari call faciality. Drawing on the portraiture tradition, the film's interviews with family members, friends and political allies trace out the contours and features of Mabo's personality. We learn that he was 'family-orientated', 'generous', 'humorous' 'egotistical' and 'proud'. These testimonies are inter-cut with numerous family snaps and other sources of photographic close-ups of Mabo's face, including footage from *Land Bilong Islanders* (1990), a film Graham and Mabo co-produced in the late 1980s. Together, these techniques 'flesh out', as one reviewer puts it, a recognisable face for the hitherto faceless name.[ix] At times the film brings us so relentlessly close to the face that we find ourselves, like ancient physiognomists, scrutinising Mabo's facial features for signs of his true nature. Certainly this is what film critic Evan Williams does when he concludes that '... in that magnificent broad countenance, with its grey, wiry mane, there was something of the sage, the prophet, the visionary. He looked the part ... (of a hero-martyr)'.[x]

The idiom of biography is also employed to give Mabo a face. Combining media reports and archival images with the interviews mentioned before, the first two-thirds of the film tells Mabo's life story in more or less chronological order. The film itemises and organises selected events from Mabo's life into a single, defining narrative of the self – 'Island Man'. Documenting Mabo's founding role in the Black Community School and his involvement in other indigenous organisations, such as the Aboriginal Legal Aid Service and the Aboriginal Medical Service, the film recounts Mabo's life as a committed activist, thus mediating public recognition of him as an influential and respected Indigenous leader. Most importantly, the film represents Mabo's relation to his island home, Mer.[xi] This is done predominately through extensive use of footage from *Land Bilong Islanders* – the film Graham made with Eddie Mabo, and which is the only audio-visual documentation of the historic *Mabo* hearings held on Mer.

But while the film is very much a social biography, we should not forget that this genre is based on the concept of the moral subject. In *Confronting Death*, David Wendell Moller describes some of the historical patterns in rituals of bereavement in Western cultures, including the emergence of biography as a particular way of recognising the rich, the pious and the brave in death.[xii] He explains how by the end of the eleventh century the idea of universal, collective destiny in death had disappeared, to be replaced by the emerging concept of biography. Recorded on the deceased's headstone as an epitaph, the biography was, in Moller's words, '... the composite picture of the choices made between good and evil' (7). Traces of this moral dimension of the genre emerge in the film's narrative depiction of Mabo as David, fighting the Goliath-like Australian legal system. One of the lawyers for the claimants testifies that Mabo conceived of himself this way. But the film is not a hagiography. To the contrary, the portrait painted of Mabo as leader-saint is tempered by revelations of his so called 'vices'. We learn that at certain times in his life, Mabo drank heavily. There is also mention of periods in his life when he was deeply depressed, as well as occasions in which he became violent.

As with all social biographies, the use of a singular narrative of self as a representation of the social/cultural narrative is achieved by seeking origins of determining aspects of self in selected events and circumstances. We are, for example, told that the origin of Mabo's fighting spirit lies in his childhood experience of growing up on Mer. He is remembered by several interviewees as a rebellious, questioning child. There is also a sequence in the film where historians, Noel Loos and Henry Reynolds, present competing claims about which event in Mabo's life gave rise to the now famous land claim. For Loos, it was the death of Mabo's father, while Reynolds inserts himself into history by suggesting it was a provocation on his part that incited Mabo to initiate the claim. The film's director leans more toward Loos' theory. What concerns me here, however, is not the question of *which* event or period in Mabo's life is the true origin of the land case, but rather how the biographical act of attributing intentionality to events and actions gives the film a specific kind of authority that derives from the conceit of allowing the dead to speak.

In his essay, 'Autobiography as De-facement', Paul de Man argues that the epitaph is not only a biographical statement but a creation of the 'fiction' of prosopopoeia – that is, the fiction that the dead subject speaks his or her mind, his or her intentions.[xiii] He claims that to address the dead is to posit the possibility of a reply and thereby confer upon them 'the power of speech': 'Voice assumes mouth, eye, and finally face, a chain manifest in the etymology of the tropes' name, *prosopon poien*, to confer a mask or face (*propson*)' (926). He argues that autobiography, like the epitaph, '... is the trope by which (...) one's name is made as intelligible and memorable as a face' (926). As prosopopoeia, this film gives the name 'Mabo' a face and in doing so confers upon the name the power of speech. This double move 'authorises' the biography as the words of the dead: 'This is Eddie's story', says Graham. But, as de Man warns, just as the trope gives a face to the dead, it can also deface the living. For de Man, the double moves of the trope – replacement and substitution – constitute a figure of 'reading as de-facement' (927). De Man argues that the illusion of prosopopoeia is always unmasked in the process of reading. He writes, 'by making death speak, the symmetrical structure of the trope implies, by the same token, that the living are struck dumb, frozen in their own death' (928). This discourse, intended to compensate for death and loss, becomes 'our actual entry into the frozen world of the dead' (928). De Man concludes that 'reading as de-facement' shows that art cannot, as it is thought to do in the Romantic tradition, substitute for forms of physical deprivation and disfigurement. As a repetition of the loss it seeks to conceal, art is also already a restoration of mortality. We saw how this happens in the previous chapter in Dennis Potter's bid for immortality. Here, as an attempt to give 'Mabo' a face, Graham's biographical film inadvertently reproduces and thus endlessly repeats the loss of face it seeks to conceal, that is, the violent severing of Eddie Mabo's name from his face/person by the cultural act of over-naming.

II: The Violence of Defacement

About three quarters of the way into *Mabo – Life of an Island Man*, the metaphoric defacement of' 'Mabo' that the film seeks to compensate for is suddenly literalised in the shocking image of a racist attack on Eddie Mabo's grave. This attack occurred in June 1995, immediately following a Torres Straight Islander tombstone unveiling ceremony held in Townsville to commemorate Eddie Mabo and to celebrate the High Court judgement.[xiv] We learn that while indigenous and non-indigenous members of Mabo's community joined together with representatives from federal and state governments in a cultural celebration, unknown attackers spray-painted Mabo's grave with racist graffiti, including two large swastikas and the racist epithet, 'Abo'. The attackers also prised a life-size bust of Mabo from its central position on the headstone, leaving in its place a large gash in the otherwise smooth, black marble surface. In an interview after the release of the film, Graham describes his personal response to the attack thus: '(I) was ... absolutely horrified and devastated ... I fell into a crumbling heap'.[xv] He also explains that the desecration of the grave is the 'real reason' for making the film: 'Bonita (Eddie's wife) was pestering me to go and film the tombstone opening ... so I got a crew together who went up to Townsville to film the tombstone opening and the celebrations. Then, of course, the day after the grave was trashed ... the real reason for making the second film was a sense of outrage about his grave being trashed.[xvi] At this point in the film we discover that the defacement of Mabo's grave is in fact the true origin of the film. And in the light of this image of actual defacement, the film's stated aim of 'giving the name a face' takes on deeper significance.

As an attack on the sacredness of the dead, defacement of a grave is a powerful act of hate. In 1990, graves in the Jewish cemetery at Carpentras, France, were attacked by a small group of anti-Semitic demonstrators. One hundred thousand people gathered in Paris to protest. They marched through the streets of Paris, joined by the then president, Francois Mitterrand. But while in France the racist attack on Jewish graves sparked widespread direct action, here, in Australia, the attack on Mabo's gave was swiftly subsumed in a struggle of competing ideologies or what Graham aptly describes as 'a media battle of symbols'. In *The Daily Telegraph Mirror* conservative columnist Piers Akerman claims that the defaced grave represents 'a wedge between black and white', the embodiment, in his mind, of the Native Title Act.[xvii] The *Australian* takes a more personal approach, using a large photograph of Bonita Mabo and her two grandsons crouched on the edge of the defaced grave to complete its neo-liberal point of view of the family as tragic victims. What we might call a 'metropolitan' point of view, *The Australian* report takes a strong moral stance only to locate the cause of the attack 'elsewhere', namely in rural Australia, in the deep recesses of the psyche's of 'a handful of racists'.[xviii]

Graham's film actively engages in this battle of symbols. In its documentation of the unveiling ceremony, the commanding, black marble headstone is framed as a symbol of the national project of Aboriginal Reconciliation.[xix] The post-colonial dream of a unified nation is captured in the figures of Bonita Mabo and Anita Keating (the latter representing the then Prime Minister, Paul Keating) reflected side by side in its shining surface. The reflective surface of the headstone serves as a mirror in which spectators can narcissistically insert themselves into a positive vision of the future. Following the attack, however, this image of unity becomes an impossible point of view. The slow pans and jerky camera movements across the disfigured grave mimic the dazed faces of those at the scene. No longer able to reflect the symbolic space of a unified nation, the defaced headstone is, literally, bereft of messages. De-metaphorised, the headstone is visible for the first time in its literal sense – that is, as a marker of the site of death. This confrontation with the physical fact of death is most powerful in the sequence of images that document the disinterment of Mabo's coffin: the sounds and images of the manual labour required to exhume the casket, the hole in the ground in Townsville's cemetery where Mabo's body once lay; the carrying away of the casket on an open trailer. From this point onward, viewing is not simply an act of social recognition but a rite of bereavement.

III: Returning Home: Mourning and Tragedy

The final section of the film is primarily a documentation of the family's renewed mourning and the re-burial of Mabo's body on his island home. Here, the narration becomes even more intimate as Graham explains that after the attack on the grave he had no choice than to continue filming. From this point onward we see that the film is very much a 'work of mourning': it repeats the scene of death as a way of working through it and inevitably moving beyond it. But it is also in this final 'act', titled, 'Journey home', that we are reminded of the close association between mourning and tragedy. The final section reproduces the devastation of the attack and subsequent reburial by way of redeeming the suffering incurred in this unexpected resurfacing of death. It does the latter by shaping the events of the attack and reburial into the easily recognisable final act of a tragedy – the Hero's Return. In *Cinema Papers*, editor and co-producer, Denise Haslem, is quoted as saying that when she and Graham were editing the film, 'they recognised that the three acts fell into a Greek tragedy so easily, there was no other way to edit it.'[xx] Following the structure of classical tragedy, the film is, its director claims, a case of 'life imitating art'. Graham is quoted as saying: '... the film is very much like the hero's journey I keep comparing it to Luke Skywalker going out to conquer the universe. He's battling the empire, but the tragedy is, unlike Luke, he dies before his great victory.'[xxi]

As a tragedy, the affective experience of this film is grounded in spectator's recognition of a generic plot structure, rendering 'the face behind the name' as the face of a tragic hero.[xxii] To see Mabo through the lens of tragedy allows us to interpret the circumstances of his death as 'dignified endurance' of an injustice, while the reburial on Murray Island becomes 'poetic justice': Mabo, who spent his life fighting for land rights, finally returns home." While this structuring of the events of Mabo's life creates a powerful and moving cinematic experience, we need also to consider the limitations of recognising Mabo in the terms of tragedy. Take, for example, Evan Williams' review. He writes: 'His (Mabo's) premature death has enshrined him as a legend, a mythic figure more potent than he was in life'. Here, Williams suggests that as with all tragic heroes Mabo is more powerful dead than alive. Indeed, Williams, goes on to suggest that had Mabo survived, had we seen him in his moment of victory, the film might not have been as good as it is. Or, to use his term, it might have been 'spoiled'. By spoiled, Williams means 'gloatingly heroic' rather than 'gentle, elegiac'. This is the thing about tragic heroes: death is not only their fate but also their nature.

As with so many others, Williams is moved by the way in which the film ends 'on a note of exquisite sadness'. Moreover, in responding to the tragic mood of the film's ending, Williams applies a popular form of cultural traditionalism that fetishises 'native custom' and 'traditions', while simultaneously erasing historical processes from contemporary forms of Aboriginal identity.[xxiii] In his interpretation of the film's ending Williams explains how 'Mabo's body is removed from its desecrated grave in Townsville and transported to Murray Island, to be buried again to the sounds of traditional music', making this a fitting ending for a tragic hero. The spectacle of the towering, turtle-shell Malo mask, combined with the dirge-like rhythms of traditional drums, enhances the drama of this act of commemoration. But to see the performance only in terms of the empty time of myth and tragedy is to overlook the historical specificity and political urgency of this cultural performance. The 'traditional music' Williams refers to is in fact the sacred Malo dance, which was performed by Murray Islanders in honour of Eddie Mabo. What the film does not tell us is that this was the first time this dance has been performed in more than 80 years (that is, nearly the entire duration of the colonisation of the Torres Strait Islands.) In her in-depth study of the *Mabo* judgement, Nonie Sharp suggests that the resurrection and performance of the Malo dance in honour of Eddie Mabo is an historic act of 'cultural revival and resistance'.[xxiv] In other words, the resurrection of this dance at this point in time is not a sign of the continuity in traditional cultural practices on Mer but rather a vivid display of the history of discontinuities resulting from colonial rule.

Likewise, by constructing the reburial of Mabo on Mer as a hero's Return, the film overlooks the fact that the state also played an important role in Mabo's 'journey home'. The then federal government funded the reburial of Mabo's disinterred body on the Murray Islands, concerned that if the grave were to remain on the mainland it could easily become an ongoing target for racist opposition to native title legislation. As Graham says in his narration, Mer is, possibly, the right place for Mabo to be buried, but for all the wrong reasons. The final shot of the film is a silent, grainy image of Mabo spear-fishing in the shallow waters that surround the island of Mer. Jeremy Beckett, cultural consultant on the film, explains that this image has specific cultural significance for the Meriam people.[xxv] But because this cultural knowledge is inaccessible to most non-indigenous spectators, spectators of this film are most likely to see Mabo as the ghostly figure of a tragic hero. In the end, the face of Mabo, which has come to stand for both the *Mabo* case and land rights in general, becomes a death mask – an image of the past consigned and *confined* to the outermost edge of the nation.

IV: The History in the Name

So far I have argued that the film's attempt to close the gap between name and face by offering us an image of Mabo as a tragic hero inadvertently re-produces the violence of de-facement. Or to put it slightly differently, as a response to an actual defacement the film's deployment of techniques of faciality becomes a form of textual de-facement: the film gives 'Mabo' a face only to render it the face of a ghost, a death mask. But there is, however, another way of seeing the film that involves opening up the gap between the name and face of 'Mabo'. In order proceed with this second approach we need to return to the origin of the film – the racist defacement of Mabo's headstone.

As with all cinematic images, the image of the defaced grave signifies more than the meanings intended by the film-makers. As many reviewers comment, this is a shocking sight, and it is the power of this image to disturb spectators that I want to examine in this second half of my analysis. Earlier, I showed how the film frames the headstone as a symbol. It is first shown as a symbol of reconciliation and later, after the attack, it is made to stand for the threat racism poses to that possibility. What I would now add to this line of argument is that the shock effect of this reproduction of the violence of defacement produces what Taussig calls 'a literalising effect'. It makes Eddie Mabo's name visible in all its nakedness *as a name* opposed, say, to a symbol or a sign for something else. In the close-up detail of the graffitied grave the name 'Mabo' becomes a scrabble of letters, setting off a series of unspeakable associations, including, for example, the play of letters between 'Mabo' and the racist epithet, 'Abo'. Before Mabo's exposed name we might also recall a body of jokes based on spellings of Eddie Mabo's name that circulated through the unofficial spaces of the pub, the taxi cab and across the back fence at the time of the *Mabo* hearings – that is acronyms such as 'MABO: Make A Better Offer', and so forth.[xxvi] We could say that the shock of the literalisation of 'Mabo' reveals the inherent strangeness of this name and, indeed, all names.

Walter Benjamin was fond of Karl Krauss' observation that 'the closer the look you take at a word, the greater the distance from which it looks back'.[xxvii] This phenomenon is never more true, I think, than on those occasions when our name is misspelt, seen out of context, attached to another, or, as in this case, under threat of obliteration. On these occasions our name stares back at us like the face of a stranger. Constructionist theories of language would tell us that what we grieve on these occasions of non-recognition is the loss of the *concept* of self. Benjamin's philosophy proposes a different view. For Benjamin, all names are a kind of death or mourning for the particularity of the thing lost in the act of naming.[xxviii] Words are 'fetishes' and, as such, there is always a difference or gap between words and the things they refer to. Which raises the question of how the particularity of things lost in the act of naming can be retrieved or, to use Benjamin's term, 'redeemed'. Not by language it seems, not by rational thought. In fact, it is Benjamin's view the truth of things cannot be made to appear. Rather, in his words, 'truth ... is revealed in a process which might be described metaphorically as the burning up of the husk as it enters the realm of ideas, that is to say a destruction of the work in which its external form achieves its most brilliant degree of illumination'.[xxix] He calls these moments of revelation 'profane illuminations', and tells an amazing story about the profane illumination of his own name in an enigmatic, fictional piece titled, 'Agesilaus Santander'.

As with the examples I gave earlier of the fleeting but, nevertheless, seismic shock we experience when we see our name emptied of its sense of self, Benjamin's story is about the revelation of such a void in the appearance of the secret name given to him by his Jewish parents. Using Gershom Scholem's translation and interpretation of this piece in his wonderful essay, 'Walter Benjamin and His Angel',[XXX] we can summarise the main ideas contained in the piece thus: Benjamin invokes the Jewish tradition of giving children a secret, magic name – a name that 'may not be entrusted or disclosed to unauthorized ones' (69) – in order to claim that mystical-religious practice for a theory of 'profane illumination'. He vividly describes a scene in which his angel, bearing his secret name, appears to him in a time of danger, as angels are supposed to do. The angel does not present him with a picture of himself as he knew himself to be. Rather, confronting his secret name in the form of a two-faced angel, Benjamin sees himself as he has not seen himself before, and is thus, 'awakened', 'transformed', 'matured' (78). The angel thus allows him to see the origin of the history of his current suffering embedded in the name.

Benjamin's conception of his angel is entirely different from the Christian conception of the guardian angel associated with biography. In the latter, the truth of the self is 'summarised' in the name. But here, as Scholem suggests, Benjamin's encounter with his angel reveals the secreted otherness of self. The encounter is also of a different temporal order to the linear time of biography. Based on a shock experience, that is, an entirely unexpected experience, the subject is jolted into a movement that, in Benjamin's words, 'pulls him into a future from which he has advanced' (58). To fully appreciate what is meant by this spatio-temporal experience, we need to know something of Benjamin's unique conception of origin. For him, the image of the origin that reveals itself in the fleeting face of the angel is not simply a repetition of the past in the present but a collision of the two that enacts a kind of double take. In *The Origin of German Tragic Drama*, Benjamin conceives the recognition of origin as an experience of seeing that which is on the one hand restored or reinstated while at the same time shows itself to be incomplete, unfinished. Or as he would later write in his 'Theses on the Philosophy of History', 'every image of the past that is not recognized by the present as one of its own concerns threatens to disappear irretrievably'.[XXXi] And in this way, the severed name is, I suggest, what Benjamin calls 'a dialectical image', an image in which 'the Then and Now come together in a constellation like a flash of lightning' to illuminate current concerns.[XXXii]

As a dialectical image, the cinematic image of Mabo's defaced headstone reveals the origin of the history embedded in the name 'Mabo'. Here, the shock effect of the image of' 'Mabo' disfigured by swastikas and the word 'Abo' renders the name faceless and unrecognisable. The name is de-personalised. But it is also true to say that having been obliterated and estranged the de-faced name *actualises* or literalises, as Taussig says, the unspeakable history of defacement that attaches to this name – that is, *terra nullius*, the original, legal form of non-recognition of indigenous law and culture upon which the Australian nation is based. In this sense, the film is not only a historical record of race hatred but a cultural performance that enables historical recognition and public memory of Australia's particular history of defacement in the form of legal non-recognition of Indigenous sovereignty. As a recurring image, the defacement of 'Mabo' takes the form of a traumatic experience. Cathy Catuth defines trauma as 'an overwhelming experience of sudden or catastrophic events, in which the response to the event occurs in the often delayed, and uncontrollable repetitive occurrence of hallucinations and other intrusive phenomena.'[xxxiii] On several occasions in this film members of Mabo's family allude to the repetitive nature of the violence of non-recognition. In an over-the-shoulder shot we see Bonita Mabo being interviewed by a young television reporter at the Townsville cemetery immediately following the discovery of the racist attack. In contrast to the image in *The Australian*, she does not appear tragic or pitiful. To the contrary, she answers the reporter's banal questions in a steeled, almost automated mode of response. When the reporter asks how the attack makes her feel, she replies: 'It's like a nightmare, starting all over again'. In a scene following this one, Mabo's son also implies that the attack on the grave is something already experienced when he explains how it has 'opened up old wounds'. History and trauma come together then as we recognise the images of defacement in this film as a traumatic presence. This trauma is, as we see, unspeakable, and it is precisely as a form of irruption in and disruption to language that the defaced name actualises the history of the effacing violence of non-recognition embedded in it.

V: The Trauma of Non-recognition

This second view of 'Mabo', in which we face the gap between the name and face rather than foreclosing it, opens the way for a different understanding of the name and naming. From this perspective, it is possible to 're-view' Mabo's life story through the lens of the history embedded in the name. As the film tells us, Mabo was born on the island of Mer, known as Murray Island, in 1936. He is the son of Robert and Paipe Sambo. When his mother died shortly after his birth, he was adopted by Benny (his maternal uncle) and Maiga Mabo. He was raised and educated on Murray Island until 1957 when the Murray Islander Council of Elders exiled him to the mainland, where he lived under two names. He was known as Eddie Mabo by most people, but also as Koiki, his Meriam (Islander) name by other Islanders and close friends.

The apparent fluidity of the name 'Mabo' was a crucial issue in the hearing of the *Mabo* case. In his commentary on the case, Beckett reminds us how the High Court's decision to recognise the collective native title rights of the Meriam people of the Murray Islands was extended to all indigenous Australians (12-13). He also brings to our attention the less known fact that Mabo's 'own claim to land was dropped in the final stages of the case' (7). This terrible irony, as Beckett refers to it, occurred because in the determination of facts and issues of the case conducted by the Supreme Court of Queensland, Justice Moynihan found Mabo's claims to be 'invalid'.[xxxiv] Moynihan concluded Mabo was not the adopted son of Benny and Miaga Mabo and, therefore, not entitled to make his claim. In addition, Moynihan believed Mabo was 'an unreliable witness' and described Mabo's explanation of Meriam inheritance custom as 'self-seeking'.[xxxv] Moynihan's refusal to recognise Mabo's land claim was in effect a refusal to recognise his name. The film implies that Mabo never recovered from the shock of this act of non-recognition. Bonita Mabo recalls her husband's reaction to this news. 'He was devastated', she says. We also learn that Mabo died a few months later, aged fifty-five. In the days leading up to his death, Mabo wrote a long, detailed genealogy of his family name.

As with the film and Beckett's commentary on the case, Nonie Sharp's cross-cultural analysis of the Murray Islander's land case defends Mabo's credibility. She analyses the extraordinary demands placed on Mabo to explain himself during the hearing of evidence in the determination of the facts and issues of the case reporting how, 'in the first fourteen days of the hearing of Eddie Mabo's evidence ... 289 objections were made by Queensland'.[xxxvi] She concludes that the demand for Mabo to explain himself, along with the subsequent non-recognition of his claim, is part of the wider trivialisation of Meriam law that occurred throughout the case. She explains how the case ignores the cultural significance of adoption and fostering of children, as well as the wider system of name holders, including the inherent code of secrecy and specific modes of oral performance of this particular system of inheritance (78). Sharp argues that when Justice Moynihan deemed Mabo's claim to be 'self serving' he was in effect refusing to recognise a crucial principle in Meriam law: to claim to own the land is 'to be responsible for it', including the responsibility of passing it on. In Meriam law, a claimant is 'a name holder on behalf of the group who are the joint owners' (78).

These kinds of suspicions and trivialisation of indigenous culture are not new. Underlining the non-recognition of Mabo's family name and the subsequent refusal of his claim to native title is the racist supposition that Mabo was not a 'proper native'. Beckett notes how many of the legal and cultural commentaries on the judgement focus on the fact that the case differentiated between Islander and Aboriginal cultures (8-10). If, however, we read the history of non-recognition *in* Mabo's name, we can see that both the Queensland Supreme Court and the High Court's treatment of Mabo are a *repetition* of the state's past treatment of Aboriginal culture and its current *reinstatement* of that attitude of suspicion in the form of the strict procedures and criteria of the Native Title Act (1993) (and its subsequent amendment in 1997.) The recent Yorta Yorta claim exemplifies the limitations of native title as a form of legal recognition. Here, Federal Court judge, Justice Olney, justified his ruling against the Yorta Yorta native title claim to land in Northern Victoria and Southern NSW by claiming that that the 'tide of history' had washed away the group's native title: 'Notwithstanding the genuine efforts of the members of the claimant group to revive the lost culture of their ancestors, native title rights and interests once lost are not capable of revival'.[xxxvii] Thus, the terrible paradox of native title: the very history the *Mabo* judgement promised to overturn is used by judges, such as Olney, to deny claimants their native title rights.

The traumatic history of non-recognition revealed in the shock of Mabo's defaced name reminds us of the material and social aspects of naming. In modern, self-oriented societies, the proper name is considered sacred. But only because it is widely regarded as equivalent to what is called 'the essence of self'. It is a view that works to conceal the inherent sociality and power of naming. It is also a view that excludes other cultural conceptions of sacredness. In the opening of his oral history, Eddie Mabo talks about his proper name as something he was 'assigned'.[xxxviii] He also explains how 'Mabo' is the name he 'grew under'. Here, the name is not given some transcendental identity to self but recognised as part of a social practice that places, obliges and even limits the bearer in relation to others. We are also reminded by Mabo's understanding of naming that, far from being primarily about notions of self, a proper name is that which entitles us to property and land rights. Not the name as a bearer of the concept of self but what Judith Butler calls, 'the action of names': to have a name is, she argues, to have the potential power to name another.[xxxix] Eddie Mabo knew this about names, and it was because of this knowledge that the Australian courts regarded him with suspicion. Graham's film portrays Mabo as activist, archivist, and an expert in colonial histories and law, all of which the courts perceived as too *white-faced*. As Beckett, observes: 'It is ironic that while anthropologists became credible expert witnesses by writing, 'natives' render themselves inauthentic by reading: tainted with literacy it seems they can't go home again!' (22). And as the film shows, Mabo did not go home again until after his death, until after his name was defaced, yet again.

VI: Face to Face

Mabo – Life of an Island Man makes Eddie Mabo recognisable to Australian audiences as a face, as *the* face of native title. But as I have tried to show in this analysis, coming face to face with another is never straightforward nor does the familiarity generated by this particular form of intimacy guarantee a non-hostile relationship. In May 1884, for instance, some five years after Queensland annexed the Torres Straight Islands, the cover of *Illustrated Sydney News* featured an etching, titled, 'Only a face at the window'. The sketch is described in the magazine thus:

> The illustration on our front page ... portrays what he (an unnamed artist) saw during a visit to an outlying station in Queensland, and which might have served for a replica of what Prout, Roberts, Fowler and others could have depicted as their experience of station life here in the early days. The Shepard's wife is preparing the damper, startled by the growl of the collie dog at her feet, looks up, and sees a lord of the soil in all his native grandeur staring in, and returns the look with one of anger and defiance. In her home she is queen, and though she knows not what danger there may be attached to the proximity of the sable visitor, she, at least, will not be the first to show any indications of fear.[xl]

'Only a face' the artist says, stripping the indigenous subject of his face, indeed, differentiating between face values. As a face-off, the colonial sketch is an early rehearsal of a mode of non-indigenous spectatorship which persists in contemporary Australian culture. It is a guarded, suspicious approach and yet one that assumes a familiarity with and intimate knowledge of the 'native' faceless subject. The editors of the *Illustrated Sydney News* suggest to us that this gaze is a 'replica' of colonial contact. In the late twentieth century and into the twenty-first, this very specific mode of spectatorship might also be regarded as a perfect replica of our juridical system's view of indigenous Australians, a view that newspaper polls indicate at least half of the Australian people are more than willing to share.[xli]

As a cultural response to the de-facement of Mabo's name, Graham's intimate style of documentary film attempts to create an opposite point of view, an entirely different mode of coming face-to-face with indigenous Australians than that depicted in the *Illustrated Sydney News*. The film seeks to mediate recognition of Mabo as a person. But there is more at stake in the defacement of Mabo's grave than depersonalisation. Graham's biographical film is circulated and widely viewed in educational contexts as *the* history of *Mabo*, albeit a special, intimate kind. In this chapter, I have argued for a reading of a different kind of intimacy than that generated by the facialising techniques employed in the film. More specifically, I have suggested that the film can be understood to generate the kind of intimacy invoked in Benjamin's piece on his (imagined) encounter with his angel, a kind of intimacy that opens the way for a different conception of the relationship between the name and face.

When Benjamin dreamed up his angel it was, as I mentioned earlier, at a time of crisis in his life. In fact, Scholem tells us the piece refers to two kinds of crisis: one personal, one political. At the time the piece was written – 1933 – Benjamin was a refugee. And it was in this desperate state, Scholem says, that Benjamin came to 'review his life through a new meditation about Paul Klee's *Angelus Novus*' – a picture that belonged to Benjamin but at the time was 'present only in his imagination' (67). He says that, for his friend, the imagined picture 'allied itself with the review of his life as writer, as Jew, and as unrequited lover' (67). But even as it revealed to him these transformations, his secret name retains what Scholem calls 'its magic character' by joining together the angelic and demonic forces of life in the most intimate union, namely, two sides of a face. For Benjamin, the secret name revealed to him in the two faces of his angel is, he writes, 'a union of the feminine and the demonic most intimately *adjacent* to each other' (59). (My emphasis). Here, adjacency implies a particular form of intimacy. As a relation founded on a shared border, the choice of the term adjacency emphasises physical proximity, while implying a nearness or closeness without conscious or psychological connection, that is, some kind of mutually recognised emotional bond. In terms of revealing a picture of himself as an unrequited lover the angel shows him how he is in a situation of being physically close to the one he loves but able to be unified with her: 'Where this man chanced upon a woman who captivated him, he was at once resolved to lurk on her path of life and wait ...' This does not that the feminine face of the angel is some kind of portrait of his unrequited lover. Rather, this face is a figuration of the specific temporality of unrequited love that requires him to wait for the lover's return. But with regard to political emancipation, this image of patience is quickly transformed into a violent image of accostment. From the demonic side of the union, Benjamin learns that it is not patience that will free him but rather a violent leap or spring, a direction that takes the form of yet another kind of adjacency. The angel, who is of course a precursor to Benjamin's 'angel of history', reveals his secret name to him by standing between past and future, and from this standpoint 'pulls him along ... into a future from which he has advanced' (59). It is a movement, a jolt to the senses, in which past and present collide in a temporary form of adjacency: a fleeting spatio-temporal collision. The history of alterity and outsiderness embedded in his secret Jewish name illuminates the origin of both of his crises: unrequited love and political exile.

Benjamin's piece on the revelation of his secret name provides us with a different way of thinking about intimacy. Moving away from a conception of intimacy as an emotional bond we find an image of intimate adjacency in which one exists in close proximity to the other but without either possession or unity – the other exists in one's orbit but is always 'beyond reach', in the way Jula Cohn and Asja Lacis were for Benjamin. This image of intimate adjacency also offers an image of the spatio-temporal dimensions of 'profane illumination' as a kind of viewing position – an experience in which past and present are jolted into a momentary collision. And considering this different kind of intimacy, which is, I believe, enabled by this film, I want to make a final comment. It is possible to view *Mabo – Life of an Island Man* as an intimate history that closes the gap between name and face, bringing us into some illusionary relation of being face-to-face with 'the man behind the name.' But it is also possible to view this film through the very gap it seeks to conceal. Taking this second perspective, we find ourselves forced to confront the underside of the mask of personalisation made visible in a series of defacements throughout the film: the gaping hole at the centre of the marble headstone where Mabo's bust was once attached, the entirely unfillable hole in the ground in Townsville's cemetery where Mabo's body was once buried, the ruptures and discontinuities to Indigenous cultural traditions as a result of colonial violence and systematic removal of Aboriginal and Torres Strait Islander peoples from their places of origin. In these defacements we can, I argue, recognise the origin of the traumatic history of non-recognition of Indigenous Australians as a violence that repeats itself today in the implementation of native title legislation, which regards Indigenous Australians with suspicion: faces at the window of the nation, looking in.

ENDNOTES

[i] For a shorter version of this chapter see my article, 'The Name and Face of Mabo: Questions of Recognition' in *Metro* 127/128, 2001. On the Mabo decision, see *Mabo –The High Court Decision, Discussion Paper, June 1993* (Canberra: Australian Government Publishing Service). Also see Noel Pearson, 'Mabo: towards respecting equality and difference' *Race Matters –Indigenous Australians and 'Our' Society*, ed. Gillian Cowlishaw and Barry Morris (Canberra: Aboriginal Studies Press, 1997); Murray Goot and Tim Rowse eds., *Make A Better Offer – the politics of Mabo* (Leichhardt, NSW: Pluto Press, 1994); W Sanders ed., *'Mabo' and Native Title: Origins and Institutional Implications* (Canberra: Centre for Aboriginal Economic Policy Research Australian National University, Research Monograph, no.7, 1994).

[ii] Jeremy Beckett, 'The Murray Island land case and the problem of cultural continuity', ed. W.S. Sanders, *'Mabo' and Native Title: Origins and Institutional Implications* (Canberra: Centre for Aboriginal Economic Policy Research Australian National University, Research Monograph, No. 7. 1994). Many thanks to Tim Rowse for drawing my attention to Beckett's article as well as Nonie Sharp's cross-cultural analysis, *No Ordinary Judgement – Mabo, The Murray Islanders' Land Case* (Canberra: Aboriginal Studies Press, 1996).

[iii] *Mabo – Life of an Island Man*, dir. Trevor Graham, dist. Film Australia, 1997.

[iv] Other film awards and nominations to date include: Third place, Certificate of Creative Excellence for the categories Documentary, Current Events, Special Events,

United States International Film and Video Festival, 1998; Finalist, Best International Documentary, 'Hot Docs', Toronto, Canada; Winner, Best Documentary Award, Australian Film Institute Awards, 1997; Winner, Best Script Award, NSW Premier's Literary Award, 1997.

[v] See: 'The Man behind the Name'(*Cairns Post*); 'Mabo family Album'(*The Daily Telegraph*); 'A Portrait of the Man who was the Mabo Case' (*The Age*) 'Mabo the Man' (*Herald Sun*) 'Powerful Portrait of Mabo'(*The Age*).

[vi] John Ryan, 'Mabo – Life of an Island Man', *Artery*, 6, no.8 (1997), 5.

[vii] Tom Ryan, 'Mabo – Life of an Island Man', *The Sunday Age* (Melbourne), 10 August 1997, C2.

[viii] Trevor Graham, *Mabo: Life of an Island Man, Original Screenplay* (Sydney: Currency, 1999), xx. It is interesting to note that this is the first documentary screenplay to be published in Australia, perhaps, the world, providing further evidence of the film's function as an historical record of *Mabo*.

[ix] Veronica Matheson, *The Sunday Herald Sun* (Melb), 'TV Extra', 9 November, 1997, p.3.

[x] Evan Williams, 'Enough redemption already', *The Weekend Australian*, 'Review', 19 July 1997, p. 11

[xi] 'Mer' is the Meriam name for the larger island in the group known as the Murray Islands in The Torres Straight. The islands were colonised by the British and annexed by the Queensland government in 1879.

[xii] David Wendell Moller, *Confronting Death: Values, Institutions, and Human Mortality* (New York and Oxford: Oxford University Press, 1996), 4.

[xiii] Paul de Man, 'Auto-biography as De-facement', *MLN*, 94 (1979), 927.

[xiv] For more detail on the unveiling ceremony and *Mabo* Day celebrations in Townsville, see Noel Loos and Koiki Mabo, *Edward Koiki Mabo: his life and struggle for land rights* (St Lucia, Qld: University of Queensland Press, 1996).

[xv] Jim Schembri, 'A portrait of the man who was the Mabo case', *The Age* (Melbourne), 30 July 1997, 7.

[xvi] Deborah Niski, 'No Man is an island', *The Sunday Age* (Melbourne), 27 July 1997, C5.

[xvii] Piers Akerman, 'Black Man's Burden', *The Daily Telegraph Mirror*, 6 June 1995, 11.

[xviii] Fiona Kennedy, 'Racists desecrate Mabo's gravestone', *The Australian*, 6 June 1995, 1.

[xix] See Michelle Gratten (ed), *Essays on Australian Reconciliation* (Melbourne: Black Inc, 2000). This excellent collection of essays offers a background to this national project, competing views on the issue, as well as the Council for Aboriginal Reconciliation's Draft Declaration of Reconciliation.

[xx] Margaret Smith, *Cinema Papers*, 119 (August, 1997), 38.

[xxi] Jim Schembri, 'A portrait of the man who was the Mabo case', *The Age* (Melbourne), 30 July 1997, 7

[xxii] Aristotle, *Poetics* (52a p. 2-4), as quoted in Stephen Halliwell, *Aristotle's Poetics* (London: Duckworth, 1986), 171.

xxiii For an excellent critique of what is identified as 'liberal racism', see Gillian Cowlishaw and Barry Morris (eds.), *Race Matters: Indigenous Australians and 'Our' Society* (Canberra: Aboriginal Studies Press, 1997).

xxiv Nonie Sharp, *No Ordinary Judgement – Mabo, The Murray Islanders' Land Case* (Canberra: Aboriginal Studies Press, 1996), 41.

xxv I am grateful to Jeremy Beckett for his response to an earlier version of this chapter and for sharing with me his first-hand knowledge of the commemorative service in Townsville, as well as his brilliant insight into the *Mabo* case.

xxvi The title of Murray Goot and Tim Rowse's *Mabo: Make A Better Offer* is intended as a play on the popular joke and as such designed to counter the derogatory insinuation that Mabo was 'self serving' in his land claims.

xxvii Karl Krauss, as quoted in Walter Benjamin, 'On Some Motifs in Baudelaire', *Illuminations*, ed. Hannah Arendt, trans. Harry Zohn (London: Fontana, 1992), 196.

xxviii Walter Benjamin, 'On Language as Such and the Language of Man', *Reflections – Essays, Aphorisms, Autobiographical Writings*, ed. Peter Demetz, trans. Edmund Jephcott (New York: Shocken Books, 1986), 330.

xxix Walter Benjamin, *The Origin of German Tragic Drama*, 31. I am grateful to Mick Taussig for drawing my attention to this passage.

xxx Two versions of this short piece from Benjamin's notebooks are translated and reproduced in Gershom Scholem's essay, 'Walter Benjamin and His Angel', *On Walter Benjamin – Critical Essays and Recollections*, ed. Gray Smith (Cambridge, Mass. and London: The MIT Press, 1995), 51-89. I am grateful to Jodi Brooks for recommending this essay.

xxxi Walter Benjamin, 'Theses on the Philosophy of History', *Illuminations*, ed. And intro. Hannah Arendt, trans. Harry Zohn (London: Fontana, 1992), 247.

xxxii See, Walter Benjamin, '"N" (Re: the Theory of Knowledge, Theory of Progress)', trans. Leigh Hafrey and Richard Sieburth, *Benjamin: Philosophy, Aesthetics, History*, ed. Gary Smith, Chicago: University of Chicago Press, 1989).

xxxiii Cathy Caruth (ed.), *Trauma: Explorations in Memory*, Baltimore and London: The John HopkinsUniversity Press, 1994. I am grateful to Jodi Brooks for recommending Caruth's work and my analysis of this scene in the film is indebted to Brooks' work on trauma and the cinema, see Jodi Brooks '"Worrying the Note": Mapping Time in the Gangsta Film," Screen 42.4 and 'Performing Aging/Performance Crisis (for Norma Desmond, Margo Channing, Baby Jane, and Sister George)', *Figuring Age: Women, Bodies, Generations*, ed. Kathleen Woodward (Bloomington: Indiana UP, 1999).

xxxiv In his judgement, Justice Moynihan wrote: 'I was not impressed with the credibility of Eddie Mabo. I would not be inclined to act on his evidence in a matter bearing on his self-interest ... unless it was supported by other creditable evidence', as quoted in Beckett, 'The Murray Island land case', 1996, 18.

xxxv Noel Loos and Koiki Mabo, *Edward Koiki Mabo: his life and struggle for land rights* (St Lucia, Qld: University of Queensland Press, 1996), 16.

xxxvi Nonie Sharp, *No Ordinary Judgement*, 1996, 41.

xxxvii See 'Native title claim "washed away"', *The Sydney Morning Herald*, 19 December, 1998, 1. For an indigenous perspective on recent developments in native title see 'Native Title and Wik: The Indigenous Position: Coexistence, Negotiation and Certainty', position paper, National Indigenous Working Group (Canberra: ATSIC, 1997).

xxxviii Loos and Mabo, *Edward Koiki Mabo*, 1996, 26.

xxxix Judith Butler, *Excitable Speech – A Politics of the Performative* (Routledge: New York and London, 1997), 28-38.

xl *Illustrated Sydney News*, 10 May 1884, 10. Many thanks to Ross Woodrow, for bringing this item to my attention.

xli See Newspoll, Saulwick and Muller and Hugh Mackay, 'Public Opinion on Reconciliation' in *Essays on Australian Reconciliation*, ed. Michelle Grattan (Melbourne: Black Inc and Bookman Press, 2000).

Video enlargement from BBC tribute to Diana Spencer (Author's collection)

Chapter 5

The Face of Diana

While I was researching this book, the death of Diana, Princess of Wales, resulted in a media event on a scale never seen before. Up until this point, I considered that perhaps Diana was *the* face of the media age. In a strange way, her death came to confirm this view. The event reached unprecedented global proportions when live television coverage of her funeral service was watched by an estimated one in three people worldwide, making it the then single most viewed event in human history.[1] Given this phenomenal degree of recognisability, it seemed that the face of Diana could be of no relevance to this study. But as the event unfolded and time passed I came to see how even the face of a media icon, a saint, no less, can become unrecognisable, making the powers of death visible when we least expect to see them.

I: The Face of a Saint

I should begin by admitting I was fascinated by Diana's face prior to her death. In fact, in that *other* Diana media event – the 1995 BBC *Panorama* interview – I found myself obsessively analysing her performance, noting her resemblance to faces of saints etched deeply in my memory as a result of a catholic upbringing. To be even more specific, I was taken in by Diana's martyr-like sufferance of calumny as an amazing imitation of the face of Joan of Arc. In death, Diana's resemblance to Joan was uncanny. Both Diana and Joan were so-called 'ordinary' women whose deaths were violent, public affairs: Joan was put to death in the spectacular medieval practice of burning at the stake, while Diana's death was, as one obituary put it, 'a horrible twentieth century, twisted metal, kind of death'. In death, both women have been patriotically 'claimed' by their respective nation states: Joan is the patron saint of France; and Diana, thanks to Elton John, has been memorialised as 'England's Rose'; she is also England's new mythic 'Lady of the Lake', laid to rest in an unmarked grave on a small island in a man-made lake on her family's estate at Althorp. At the beginning of the nineteenth century, Napoleon used images of a sword-wielding, banner-carrying maiden Joan as a symbol of a unified France. Likewise, pictures of Diana in 90s-style Perspex armour striding through minefields in Angola continue to have a unifying effect in the Red Cross campaign for an international ban on land mines. And the list goes on, raising the question of whether it merely a coincidence that these two women, who are regarded so similarly by the 'faithful' in death, have a remarkably similar countenance? Or, is it the case that their faces determine their saintly status?

The first thing we need to note about the processes of canonisation is that it is not so much a question about a person *being* saintly, but being *recognised* as such. In *Saints and Society*, Donald Weinstein and Rudolph Bell make the point that popular perception plays an important part in being recognised as a saint: 'While the church uses heroic virtue to distinguish saints from wizards and witches, in popular belief saintly virtue was less a legalistic than a charismatic matter. A combination of the force of personality, rigorous self-denial, humility and good works led people to believe that a saint was in their midst.'[ii] But while this may be the case, saintly recognisability is complicated by the fact that sainthood is by definition a state of perfection that only the saint can fully know. A saint's holiness is technically *unrepresentable*; an impossible image. In one way this fits precisely with Edith Wyschogrod's thesis on saints and postmodernity: that is, 'Not only do saints contest the practices and beliefs of institutions, but in a more subtle way they contest the order of narrativity itself'.[iii] In other words, saints trouble the basic premise of representation. For this reason, artists have turned to indirect or reflective means of depicting saints. Images of saints are not portraits – that is, images of the face as a mirror of the soul. Rather, faces of saints are emblematic of particular and easily recognisable (identifiable) Christian virtues. Saints are recognise d by the faithful as 'exemplars' – models of behaviour which the faithful are encouraged to imitate.[iv] But as George Hersey points out, although imitation is meant to take the form of spiritual transformation, the fact is that in visual culture there is an unavoidable imbrication between the spiritual and the physical,[v] setting off a mirroring effect. Becoming a saint is a process in which the faces of the saints are the same as the faces of those who imitate the saints. Or, to put it slightly differently, in order to become a saint, one must have the right kind of face.

Of course not all saints are born with the required face. Take Joan, for example: images circulating in religious and popular culture of a beautiful, brave and innocent heroine bear little resemblance to the historical figure. In fact, the truth is that not much is known about Joan's actual physical appearance. Not that this has prevented historians from speculating. It is generally considered that Joan was 'ruddy-faced', though one historian lamely interprets the absence of any descriptions of her face as a sign that she was unattractive.[vi] However, historical accuracy is not the point here. What is of most interest is the way in which a particular facial type has been *conferred onto* the historical figure of Joan. Just as I, who, as a child, read the lives of saints and prayed before statues of them in my local church, immediately recognise d Diana's presentation of self in the *Panorama* interview as an imitation of Joan, Joan herself is an imitation of female martyrs who came before her. Joan was besotted with St Catherine, claiming that she 'spoke' to her. Joan's love for St Catherine inspired St Therese of Lisieux's book on Joan, and Diana, it is reported, had a great devotion to St Therese.

In the reports of Diana's death and tributes to her life there are numerous images of her 'acting like a saint'. One example is the now famous image of her cradling an unnamed dying child at Imrahn Kahn's cancer hospital in Pakistan. In terms of perceived saintliness, many commentators of the day noted that this highly staged performance was a very good imitation of that other well-known twentieth-century female saint – Mother Teresa, who by coincidence died just two days following Diana's death, sparking an outpouring of commentaries on the similarities and differences between these media-age saints. But if, as I have suggested, saints are required to wear their virtue on their face, then Diana's youthful beauty and crafted glamour betray her performance of selflessness. It is interesting to note that while Mother Teresa's much commented on 'plain' face was on view in her death, Diana's face was kept under wraps. Mainstream media colluded to keep the only known photograph of the seriously injured Diana from public view.[vii] Hence, we might well ask what virtue we recognise d in the face of Diana. What virtue was protected by keeping alive the memory of Diana's living face? And why is Diana's saintliness more attractive than Mother Teresa's selfless piety?

James A Golden returns to Socrates' view of beauty to explain the power of Diana's face. He argues that what we recognise d in her beauty were Platonic virtues of the Good: dignity, humility, mildness, good nature. He quotes a British journalist, who, at the time of Diana's death, wrote the following: 'The Princess' captivating beauty was obvious from the moment she came to public attention. What changed over the years was her ability to project her beauty [in such a way that she became] a powerful figure-head for charities and campaigns'.[viii] But such 'true' goodness was not always recognise d. It is interesting to note how in many of the reports immediately following her death, Diana's often maligned, emotional and direct style of responding to situations – 'I touch people. I believe everyone needs to be touched' – was suddenly redeemed as a saintly virtue. Journalists and commentators who once criticised Diana for her naivety, such as the time she shook the hand of a dying AIDS patient in full view of the world's news cameras, now claimed that her innocent, direct approach was an appropriate, if not exemplary mode of response to the world's complex problems.

As with Joan, Diana's perceived saintliness or if you like, goodness, derived from her ability to project the quality of innocence.[ix] But being perceived as innocent involves more than having a youthful, sweet-faced appearance. Innocence is associated with artlessness. We assume, for example, that the expression on the face of a child is an unmediated expression of their state of mind. The innocent face is considered to be fully open and hence, absolutely legible. For this reason we find that in visual art, the expression of innocence is fixed in delicate child-like facial features. François Rude's romantic sculpture of Joan as a girl with far-away eyes is a good example of such an expression. However, in the age of the moving camera, the task of 'capturing' the virtue of innocence in a mobile face is more difficult. Many films have been made about Joan of Arc, including French director, Luc Besson's, 1999 version, featuring the well-known US actor Dustin Hoffman playing God, no less. But many critics agree that the best cinematic depiction of Joan's story is Carl Dreyer's 1928 silent film, *La Passion de Jeanne d'Arc*.[x] Consisting nearly entirely of close-ups of the faces of Joan and her persecutors, the film is, as one critic describes it, an 'orchestration of faces'.[xi] Dreyer does not, however, try to get 'inside' Joan's head. Rather he spiritualises Joan's face by making it relentlessly and intensively express the affects of the pain and humiliation of torture and persecution. In other words, in this film Joan's holiness is perceived in the extraordinary performance of physical pain and mental confusion she endured.

Like the actor Maria Falconetti, who brilliantly performed the face of Joan in Dreyer's film, Diana was a master in the art of facial expression, as seen in the 1995 *Panorama* interview. The interview was a clever defence of her position in the Royal family. Instead of attacking her 'enemies', Diana 'confessed' her sins, and in so doing so, redeemed herself in the eyes of her beloved public. The success of her presentation lay in the expression of her pain and personal suffering. This was achieved in part through her self-characterisation as an innocent child who had suffered at the hands of uncaring adults, including her husband, his family, her lovers and, of course, her parents. Diana's self-infantalisation was also expressed in her face: uncharacteristic dark eye make-up and flat pink lipstick gave her a dramatic tragic quality. Her head, tilted downward and held slightly to one side added to the appearance of child-like timidity, while throughout the interview Diana's eyes welled with tears, and her trademark upward glance sealed her innocent appeal.

To what degree Diana's performance in the *Panorama* interview was a conscious act is not the issue. What is more important is the fact that this self-performance was widely regarded as artless and thus, authentic. In the days immediately following Diana's death images from this interview were recycled as *the* authentic image of Diana. The BBC, for example, used this image as the back-drop for their memorial special, hosted by Jonathon Dimbleby, screened in Britain the night following her death. They also used this image in their television coverage of Diana's funeral service. When the casket was being carried out of the Westminster Abbey this image suddenly appeared like a ghost in the top left-hand corner of the screen: Diana the innocent, presiding over the event of her death.

There are, I am sure, many reasons why journalists gravitated toward this image as *the* image of Diana, one being, perhaps, that of all her many faces – 'lady in waiting', 'fairytale princess', 'adoring mother', 'cover girl', etc., – the face of Diana as innocent, suffering martyr makes the most sense of her senseless death. Martyrs are not supposed to survive. In fact, death and physical suffering make them all the more glorious, more beautiful, and more useful to the living. Conscious or unconscious, sincere or insincere, the face of Diana as saint is neither a mirror to some pure and holy soul, nor that in which we might recognise ourselves. Rather, Diana's fantastic capacity for self-transformation reveals the imitative nature of sainthood, thus exposing the faces of saints as the masks they are. But more than this, to look upon the alluring, radiant face of Diana in the hope that her innocence will somehow redeem our sins, or that her eternal beauty can in some sublime way make sense of a senseless world, will surely end in disappointment. For what we discover is that this face of our age is a mirror blindly reflecting back to us an image of this world as a world of mirrors. I do not mean this is in a facile or cynical way. I want only to suggest that perhaps it is precisely this distorted, negative reflection that caught the world off guard and, for the briefest time in world history, made death visible on a scale hitherto unthinkable.

Of course the shock of this face of death was quickly recouped for other purposes: nationalism, sentimentality, profit, revenge, and so on. Two years later, collective embarrassment had set in. On the second anniversary of Diana's death, journalists declared Diana the 'forgotten princess'[xii], while public commemoration of her had considerably diminished: there was a noticeable lack of attention to the anniversary of her death in the media, the British government announced it had cancelled its plan to build a statue in her honour, there was a marked decline in visitors to the Diana museum at Althorp, and sales of the many publications on Diana had fallen.[xiii] By the fifth anniversary in 2002, there was little more than an embarrassed murmur – no official wreath-laying, no minute's silence in the Commons, no church service – leading writer, Robert Harris, to comment: 'Not since Trotsky was expelled from the Soviet Union in 1929 has a prominent public figure been so comprehensively airbrushed out of a nation's life.'

For Diana's brother, Earl Spencer, the disappearance of Diana image from British public life is part of larger, ongoing conspiracy. In the only interview given on the occasion of the fifth anniversary, he claimed: 'I think there was a feeling among those who were never Diana's supporters of "let's marginalise her and tell people she never mattered and tell people that in the first week of September 1997 they were all suffering from mass hysteria"'.[xiv] It is tempting to see the official erasure of Diana in terms of class conflict – that is, as an erasure of the common experience. But more significantly, I think, this forgetfulness confirms that Diana's death is emblematic of death in general in the media age. In 2002, memory of the spectacular event of Diana's death is overshadowed by media events leading up to the first anniversary of the September 11 terrorist attack on the World Trade Building (more analysis of these reports is provided in the afterword). In this way, the increasingly forgettable face of Diana shows not that we have become blasé about death, but that death is increasingly experienced only as an image. And, as with all images, the face of Diana is not durable, eternal. Rather it exists only as it is recognised, and in the media age, recognisability is short-lived.

II: Forgotten Princess

In *The Colour of Time: Claude Monet*, Virginia Spate explains how Monet's 'automatic' response to the death of his beloved wife Camille was to paint a picture of her dead face. Spate contends that Monet's action should not be interpreted as a desire to document his wife's existence, nor to record her 'true' nature, in the tradition of the death-mask or commemorative portrait.[xv] Rather, relying on an account of this event by Monet's friend Georges Clemenceau in which the artist describes his response as 'mechanical', she convincingly argues that we should see the painting of the dead Camille as emblematic of Monet's mode of seeing. According to Clemenceau, Monet describes this mode thus:

> the obsession, the joy, the torment of my days, to the extent that one day, seated at the bedside of a dead woman (his first wife) who had been and still was very dear to me, I surprised myself with my eyes fixed on her tragic forehead, in the act of mechanically observing the succession, the encroachment of fading colours which death was imposing on the immobile face ... That's what I had come to. It's quite natural to wish to reproduce the last image of one who is about to leave us forever. But even before I had the idea of recording the features to which I was deeply attached, my bodily organism reacted in the first place to the shocks of colour, and in spite of myself my reflexes drew me into an unconscious process in which the daily round of my life was resumed. Just like an animal on a treadmill...xvi

As I said, Spate claims that the painting of the dead Camille is exemplary of what she calls Monet's 'bleak objectivity'. She also shows how in his determination to represent 'certain aspects of the visible world as truthfully as he could', Monet restricted himself to moments with no past and no future (7). In this way, Spate's critique challenges the Realist perspective routinely overlayed onto Monet's work. She convincingly argues that Monet's objectivity creates 'images of the external world embodying his processes of shaping it into his own'. Or, as she suggests, the paintings betray Monet's wish to cease the flow of the rapid disappearance of pre-industrial culture. In this way, Spate makes the brilliant critical move of placing Monet's work in the context of industrialisation and the social change taking place in late nineteenth-century Europe. And this is a similar line of thinking to that which Kracauer takes when he accounts for modern image-hunger evidenced in the popularity of the illustrated magazine as a repression or concealment of a greater fear of death and destruction.

In a catalogue accompanying the exhibition of the Beyler collection, the entry on Monet's *'Rouen Cathedral: the portal (morning) 1894'* notes that the painting is part of an extensive series in which Monet demonstrated 'an object mutating; its appearance transformed by the changing light'. Following Spate, we could say that the vision of sensuous plenitude – as this image is in all its glorious blues and mauves and wash of light – bares traces the same mechanical mode of seeing that Monet experienced before the face of his dead wife. In her analysis of this painting and the series it comes from, Spate invokes Walter Benjamin when she describes Monet's desire to get closer and closer to the object as a proximity that results in the object's near disintegration. While most critics saw Monet's interest in the cathedral in terms of an interest in the durability of form, Spate argues otherwise. She writes: '... while the form of the facade remained constant through every change of light, the repeated rendering of it profoundly undermined its reality, and its "durable nature" became ambiguous, fugitive, fragmentary'. Or as Monet himself once claimed 'everything changes, even stone'.[xvii]

My point is that Monet approached the Cathedrals of Rouen in much the same way he approached the face of his dead wife: with a sense of urgency associated with his a fear of not capturing something before it disappears. And it is interesting to note that in this same year that Monet mourned the loss of pre-industrial France in a series of images of architectural de-formation, the world was introduced to cinema – that cultural form of visual shock that both Benjamin and Kracauer argue can force a spectator to confront the transitory nature of existence through its unique capacity to capture the physiognomical aspects of things. To see people and things in their process of material disintegration *as an image* creates uneasiness within the spectator. And as Miriam Hansen argues 'It is in such moments of almost physical recognition that Kracauer grants photography the potential to offer an antidote to its own positivist ideology, its complicity with the social repression of death'.[xviii]

Seen from this perspective, Diana's death unleashes the very uneasiness that 'the blizzard' of images of people like herself normally distract us from. As with the rapid and mechanical response by Monet to the sight of his dead wife, we can note the incredible speed with which the world's media responded to news of Diana's death. Here I am thinking of the way in which Western television networks and press produced elaborate photographic and televisual memorials to her within less than twenty-four hours of her death. This speed is of course only equivalent to the acceleration of processes by which techniques of reproduction increasingly influence our existence in general. It is also arguable that this speed was possible only because Diana already was, as I explained earlier, an image, a media icon. In death, the face of Diana became a time-image, revealing the peculiar qualities of late twentieth-century media time.

Five years later, the image of Diana continues to serve this purpose, although now it reveals a different aspect of contemporary forms of temporality. In recent times we have seen how just as rapidly as Diana became *the* image of the late twentieth century, she has now become a striking image of the outmoded. Or to use a phrase Kracauer applies in his analysis of a photograph of his grandmother in his essay 'Photography', the face of Diana 'no longer belongs to our time'.[xix] Today, Diana's image is superseded by others, including her sons'. Most recently her youngest son marked the anniversary of his 18th birthday by publicly announcing that he would follow in his mother's footsteps, carrying on with her charitable work. Television reports of this announcement brought us pictures of Prince Harry in the corridors of Ormond Street hospital in London where his mother also held many of her famous press conferences. This uncanny image became doubly uncanny when a hospital worker handed Harry a framed picture of his mother. Here, the recycled image of Diana as tireless charity worker – the face of a modern day saint – appears empty and lifeless. No longer referring to the woman who once existed, it has become a truly dead object – a souvenir of a time past. As Harry distractedly fumbles the image of his mother we see that it is not yet a ruin, and therefore has none of the sacred status associated with long past time. On the contrary, the face of Diana has become a representation of the recent past. And as Kracauer observes in his essay on photography, 'the recent past that claims to be alive is more outdated than that which existed long ago and whose meaning has changed'. (430) And just as Kracauer suggests that images of the recent past are often the most comical, I had to admit to myself that the reproduction of Diana's forlorn face in this recent news report appeared nothing less than ridiculous.

The deep sense of shock experienced by millions of people around the world upon hearing about the death of Diana has long since dissipated. The intensity of the mass outpouring of grief that followed this news is utterly expended. But looking back, those few days in September 1997 when it seemed that the entire whole world mourned the death of Diana are, surely, more than cause for embarrassment. Rather than reduce this global cultural phenomenon to 'mass hysteria' we might instead reflect on the way in which the media event of Diana's death set-off a deep, collective experience of facing death. As a mass experience of the death of an image, and, conversely, an experience of death *as an image*, the event of Diana's death reveals the way in which modern image hunger conceals death through its complex logics of speed; in media culture a face can become instantly recognisable only to become unrecognisable in equally rapid time.

ENDNOTES

[i] This chapter is based on a commentary I published shortly after the death of Diana. See Therese Davis, 'The Face of a Saint', *Planet Diana: Cultural Studies and Global Mourning*, ed. Re-public (Nepean, NSW: Research Centre in Intercommunal Studies, 1997). Also see Ivor Gaber, 'Some Reflections on the Television Coverage of Diana, Princess of Wales', *Papers from An Era of Celebrity and Spectacle: The Global Rhetorical Phenomenon of the Death of Diana, Princess of Wales, A Trilogy of Conferences*, ed. Gregory J. Payne (Boston: Centre for Ethics in Political and Health Communication, 2000).

[ii] Donald Weinstein and Rudolph M. Bell, *Saints and Society: Two Worlds of Western Christendom, 1000-1700* (Chicago and London: University of Chicago Press, 1984), 143.

[iii] Edith Wyschogrod, *Saints and Postmodernism* (Chicago: University of Chicago Press, 1990), 88.

[iv] See Paola Tinagli, *Women in Italian Renaissance Art: Gender, Representation, Identity* (Manchester and New York: Manchester University Press, 1997).

[v] See George L. Hersey, *Sexual Selection From the Medici Venus to the Incredible Hulk* (Cambridge, Massachusetts: MIT Press, 1996).

[vi] See Henri Guillemin, *Joan, Maid of Orleans*, trans. Harold J. Salemson (New York: Saturday Review Press, 1977).

[vii] Copies of a photograph of an injured Diana, taken by one of the paparazzi who were following Diana at the time of the fatal crash, were posted on the Internet within hours of her death were not to my knowledge published in mainstream press.

[viii] James A. Golden, 'The Life and Death of Princess Diana: A British Philosophical/Rhetorical Perspective', *Papers from An Era of Celebrity and Spectacle: The Global Rhetorical Phenomenon of the Death of Diana, Princess of Wales, A Trilogy of Conferences*, ed. Gregory J. Payne (Boston: Centre for Ethics in Political and Health Communication, 2000), 238.

[ix] See Marina Warner, *Joan of Arc: The Image of Female Heroism* (London: Vintage, 1981). Warner argues that Joan's perceived innocence was crucial to cultural conceptions of her as a female hero.

[x] See Mark Nash, *Dreyer* (London: BFI Publishing, 1977). See also Marsha Kinder and Beverle Houston, 'The Passion of Joan of Arc (1928)', *Close-Up: A Critical Perspective on Film* (New York: Harcourt, Brace, Jovanovich, 1972): 44-48.

[xi] Nash, *Dreyer*, 11.

[xii] Warren Hoge, 'Two Years On, Diana Is the 'Forgotten Princess'', *New York Times*, 1 Sept., 1999, A4.

[xiii] See Seth Stevenson, 'Goodbye, Di', *Newsweek* (US), 6 Sept., 1999, 11.

[xiv] Earl Spencer, in *The Guardian*, as cited in Paul Daley 'Why Diana can't rest in peace' *The Sydney Morning Herald*, Weekend Edition, 24-25 August 2002, p31.

[xv] Virginia Spate, *The Colour of Time: Claude Monet* (London: Thames and Hudson, 1992), 7.

[xvi] As quoted in Spate, *The Colour of Time: Claude Monet*, 7.

[xvii] Spate, *The Colour of Time: Claude Monet*, 225, 231.

xviii Miriam Hansen, '"With Skin and Hair": Kracauer's Theory of Film, Marseille, 1940'. *Critical Inquiry*, 19 (1993), 456.

xix Siegfried Kracauer, 'Photography' (1927), trans. Thomas Y. Levin, Critical Inquiry, 19 Spring 1993, p.423.

REMEMBER
ME

Michael F. Lynch

Video enlargement from ABC TV News (Author's collection)

Chapter 6

Remembering the Dead: Faces of Ground Zero

Frances Yates' influential study of the art of memory begins with an anecdote that goes something like this: At a banquet given by a nobleman of Thessaly named Scopas the poet Simonides of Ceos recites a lyric poem in honour of his host but includes a passage in praise of the twin gods, Castor and Pollux. Scopas is furious. He tells the poet that he will only pay him half the sum agreed upon for the poem, and that he must obtain the balance from Castor and Pollux. A short while later, a message is brought in to Simonides that two young men are waiting outside who wish to see him. He rises from the banquet and goes out. But the poet finds no one. Alas, during his absence the roof of the banqueting hall falls in, crushing Scopas and all the guests to death beneath the ruins; the corpses are so mangled that the relatives who come to take them away for burial are unable to identify them. But Simonides saves the day. He remembers the places at which the dead had been sitting at the table and is, therefore, able to indicate to the relatives which are their dead.[i]

For Yates, this story, which was first cited in Cicero's lessons in rhetoric (*de Oratore*), demonstrates how from its inception the art of memory relies upon a good sense of spatial order. As Yates notes, '... it was through his memory of places that the guests had been sitting that [Simonides] had been able to identify the bodies, he realised that orderly arrangement is essential for good memory' (2). The anecdote also demonstrates the powerful association between memory and death. Here, in its 'original' application the art of memory is a weapon against death's power to make the dead unrecognisable and thus undermine the sovereignty of the individual. But as a cultural response to this act destruction, the art of memory not only allows us to continue to recognise the dead, but also makes the world of the dead as stratified as the world of the living, in that it involves remembering the proper, let's say social, place of those who have died. And in this regard, some faces are more memorable than others.

I: Disaster, Terrorism and Television

Fast-forwarding from the ancients to the age of terrorism, we discover that television plays a crucial role as a site of public memory and memorialisation in the face of large-scale disaster. This is more than ironic, for many argue that television is, if not the cause of terrorism, then certainly a major contributing factor to increases in terrorist activities.[ii] In 1946 a militant Zionist group orchestrated an elaborate plan to bomb the British military and administrative headquarters in the south wing of the luxurious King David Hotel in Jerusalem. As seen in the television documentary *The Age of Terrorism*, British newsreel footage of the aftermath of the Jerusalem Bomb is uncannily reminiscent of media reports of the devastation caused by the terrorist attacks on the World Trade Center in New York on September 11, 2001.[iii] In terrorism studies, the Jerusalem Bomb, as it is known, marks the beginning of terrorism as a media event, actions designed to capture the world's attention. In the past 40 years or more television has become the main field in which terrorist acts of this kind are played out. As Walter Laqueur explains: 'Guerilla warfare can exist without media coverage, but for terrorism publicity is absolutely essential, and the smaller the terrorist gang the more it depends on publicity. This is one of the reasons ... why terrorism occurs in some countries and not others. Under a totalitarian regime ... a terrorist group will find it exceedingly difficult to get organized in the first place. Even if against all odds, it should succeed in doing so, its exploits would not normally be reported in the media and this, of course, would defeat the whole purpose of the exercise – *the deed would pass unheralded and unrecognized*' (my emphasis).[iv] The demand by terrorist groups for recognition has led to what some authors call a 'symbiotic' relation, or as one critic, Martin Essler calls it, 'an organic connection', between modern terrorism and the nature of television.[v] Here, Essler is referring to not only television's status as the principal information medium in the twentieth century, but also its unique properties, such as liveness and immediacy, as well as what many refer to as television's 'entertainment value', that is, its practice of dramatising local and world events. As Essler argues: 'the drama, the intensity of the suspense, and the ongoing news potential of the unfolding events that actions such as embassy takeovers and hostage taking provide give the perpetrators of these acts an almost ideal field for publicizing themselves, especially when the moment for the final assault on hostage exchange arrives and everything is in place and can be fully and minutely shown on the TV screen' (63-64).

Writing some twenty years ago, Essler was responding to the then increasingly spectacular reports of terrorist bombings, hijackings, sieges and hostage taking, such as the Iranian hostage crisis of 1979 and the siege of the Iranian Embassy in London. In these cases, what Essler and others claim about terrorism and television is correct: television in these instances is able to show viewers the events as they unfold in all their minute detail. Gaye Tuchman in *Making News: A Study of the Construction of Reality* refers to this kind of terrorist act as 'the developing kind'.[vi] In November 1979, for example, Euro-American television networks broadcast pre-planned images of militant Iranians parading blindfolded, shackled American hostages in the streets of Tehran. In a study of recent developments in the relation between television and terrorism, Menahem Blondheim and Tamar Liebes distinguish between this type of media event 'featuring the deliberate staging and dramatic coverage of pre-planned symbol-laden moments in the social process' and a second genre they call 'the disaster marathon'.[vii] The latter is differentiated by the element of surprise: 'in disaster marathons television is not pre-warned, and in most cases cannot fathom that it could happen' (275). Like other critics in this field, Blondheim and Liebes argue that what they call the disaster marathon genre and live broadcasting are interdependent.[viii] Television coverage of Gulf War II in 2003, for example, saw the introduction of specialist techniques and practices in this area, such as 'live streaming' – unedited footage – and 'embedded reporters' – television journalists and their crews attached to front line troops for the purpose of capturing and transmitting vision of surprise events.[ix] In these instances it is, as Blondheim and Liebes remark, 'increasingly difficult to distinguish ...between television's coverage of an event and its becoming part of it' (274).

In both of these genres of reporting on terrorism the violence of the terrorist act is expressed most sensationally in and through close-ups of the bodies of victims. In the case of developing types of events, such as hostage taking, television cameras zoom in on the bodies and faces of the captives. As with Simonides, television also plays a role in identifying the often unrecognisable faces and bodies of victims of terrorist attacks. In 1979 American network television provided viewers with detailed profiles of the American hostages, along with interviews with family members and friends. But, of course, not all victims of terrorism are made recognisable. In his commentary on Euro-American television coverage of disasters in Africa, Kwame Karikari explains '[w]hen there is mayhem in Africa or other places, CNN or BBC shows you the broken limbs, the dead bodies, and the vultures feeding on them, the gore and the blood. They show you human suffering. They show you helplessness. In Africa, when violence goes berserk, however, what the BBC and the CNN rarely, if ever, show you is an African mother weeping, wailing, shedding tears'.[x] Television's coverage of the bodies of victims of terrorist acts, indeed, its role in the structuring of the modern mediated terrorist act, needs be understood in a global context. Like Simonides, Euro-American broadcasters attribute face value when they identify victims of terrorism according to the laws of social order. That is to say, as a form of public memory, the facialising techniques of television reproduce the hierarchies of world power that assign peoples of different countries their various positions at the world table.

II: Live History

The terrorist attack on the twin towers of the World Trade Center, New York, September 11, 2001 was a catastrophic event that even now commentators compete to make sense of. But whether critics see the attack as the end of postmodernism, payback for American dominance, God's judgement of American secularism or the beginning of a New World Order, they all agree that September 11 is a singular media event. In 'Notes on the Logic of the Global Spectacle' Jonathan Flatley argues that what makes September 11 unique is not the scope or nature of its destruction but the fact of its global viewing.[xi] He claims that '[i]t is possible that no other historical event has ever received such a wide public viewing during the event itself' (1). Along with others, Flatley makes the obvious but nevertheless important point that the September 11 attacks were planned in terms of their potential visual effect, or, to use his words, 'their reproducibility as images' (1). In Australia, late-night scheduling was interrupted by images of one of the WTC towers in flames. Drawn in by the spectacular and curious quality of this report, I watched as network news anchors speculated about the how and why of what was at that point presumed to be a disastrous accidental plane crash. I remember the strangeness of the image of billowing smoke filling what was an otherwise glorious blue sky. I also remember seeing the second plane enter the field of vision and, as with television commentators, thinking it must be part of some kind of rescue mission. When the second plane hit the second tower my shock was immediate. It was also in synchronization with the shock experience of the broadcasters who were also desperately trying to make sense of what they had seen. In this moment, my viewing contributed to a global collective experience of disbelief. My viewing was no longer a matter of being fascinated by the spectacle of disaster. Rather, I was suddenly implicated in an historical event that was unfolding on the screen before my eyes, a disaster which I had 'witnessed' live but had no unmediated connection to. That is to say, I had no means of connection to the event other than as spectator.

As time passed, live television transmitted image after image of the unfolding event. Within what seemed like minutes after the second crash, Tower One appeared to explode and then collapse. There were also the unthinkable images of people jumping from the tower followed by the sight of the explosion and collapse of the second tower. The collective shock and disbelief generated by this televised event is, perhaps, best expressed in the words of an eyewitness, Captain Dennis Tardio, interviewed by French film directors Jules and Gedeon Naudet. Filmed on site that first night, a traumatised, bewildered Tardio signals toward the space where the WTC towers once rose above other buildings and says, 'They're not there! It's hard to believe. You look, but they're not there.' Later, back at the fire station, Tardio asks the question: 'It did happen, right? It's not something like I'm going to close my eyes and open them again to see the towers? It's not there, right?'.[xii] And then we watch as he shakes his head over and over.

This deep sense of disbelief distinguishes September 11 from television coverage of 'developing types' of terrorist acts. In this case, television was not 'in place' to record events. Just the opposite, television and its viewers were caught off guard and unprepared. In this way, September 11 is exemplary of what Blondheim and Liebes call the disaster marathon, which is distinguished from the other genre by the element of surprise. These authors argue that there are several significant consequences associated with the element of surprise: 'This element of surprise, inherent in disaster marathons, underscores its diametrically opposite relationship with the establishment. If in media events the political establishment takes over the media and the public, during disasters forces external to the political establishment capture the attention of media and public' (275). Blondheim and Liebes claim that the chaos created in the aftermath of a terrorist instigated disaster, including disruption to routine of any kind, opens a space for perpetrators to control the event: 'In the disaster marathon's routine, once television's news editors are pushed to open-ended live coverage, they discover they have no 'script'. Large-scale disasters have no ascribed symbolic closure: their broadcast cannot resonate with a salient, integrative social credo, nor provide either immediate or long-term solutions. Their script, in effect, comes under the control of the perpetrators. The chaotic, improvised nature of the disaster marathon telecast amplifies the terrorists' intent to produce uncertainty, instability, and anxiety' (275). It is true that the perpetrators' actions on September 11 led to an unprecedented lack of control by the establishment. And as Blondheim and Liebes admit, the American state's scramble to gain control of the situation in New York and Washington was undermined by a series of unexpected 'absences' or omissions that served to prolong the sense of uncertainty and, I would argue, the deep sense of disbelief that is associated with trauma.

On the day after the attacks, Euro-American network cameras that encircled the site now known as Ground Zero focussed their long-range lenses on the hundreds of ambulance and other emergency service crews waiting to apply triage and assist in rescue operations. But as time passed, it became evident there were no survivors to be rescued, let alone treated. Television provided images of rubble, mattered bent steel, smoke, dust, fire, crushed vehicles, empty streets, smashed glass, mud and all sorts of other debris. But there were no bodies. As with the experience of disbelief described by the firefighter chief when he looks into the sky only to discover that the towers are no longer there –'You look, but they're not there' – television viewers like myself waited and watched for survivors, but 'they were not there'. In fact, after twenty-four hours of frantic digging and shifting by hundreds of workers there was only one survivor. As one firefighter recalls in his account of this first day after the attack: 'Guys were digging fast, frantically. We'd be digging and then all of a sudden people would yell "Quiet!" And the whole place would get quiet and people would look, calling 'Hello'. And then slowly they would go back to work and start digging again. That's how things went down there.'[xiii]

In the days that followed commentators talked endlessly, wrote page after page of writing about the event, while television news endlessly repeated its Hollywood-style montage of images of the attack and the collapsing towers (Note: It's not that the images *resembled* a Hollywood disaster movie, as so many claim, but that within minutes of being captured this vision was edited to resemble a Hollywood disaster movie). But the point is, all this talk, all these printed words, all the replays of the sight of the towers collapsing could not cover over the silence and/or fill the absent space of the site now known as Ground Zero. Nor could this information overload distract us from the facelessness of the perpetrators. Unlike most terrorist acts where perpetrators make themselves visible in order to demand recognition for their movement or cause, the perpetrators of September 11 remained anonymous. Even when American intelligence pointed the finger at Osama Bin Laden, and Western media flooded the world with images of his face, he remained silent, elusive. Not even the subsequent war in Afghanistan could produce Bin Laden's body. Apart from a few video glimpses, Bin Laden is to this day what WJT Mitchell describes as 'a ghostly figure, a spectral image that can't be killed'.[xiv]

III: Nothing to Mourn

In its coverage of the September 11 terrorist attack, television was much more than an information service. By inadvertently making us aware of the absences, silences and omissions of the event, television 'replays' the ultimate horror of terrorism: namely, the threat of total oblivion, of nothing to mourn. As the site of a global experience of absence, an anxiety about not seeing, Ground Zero marks what Jacques Derrida (in another context) calls 'the loss of the archive', taking the threat associated with terrorism to another level.[xv] In his discussion of the nuclear imagination, Derrida argues that the fundamental threat is that there will be no social remainder left to remember, nothing or no one to mourn. This is the level of anxiety reached at the peak of the media event of September 11. These attacks mark a profound shift in the West's imagination of terrorism. Firstly, for the obvious reason of the massive level of destruction created by this multiple target attack, about which much has been said and debated by a great many experts.[xvi] But in addition, there is also the anxiety created by our experience of seeing on television how bodies, indeed thousands of bodies, can 'go missing', how they can easily slip into the space of the unidentified, the space of facelessness and forgetfulness, or what Essler once called 'the abyss of nonhistory' (65). In other words, while the terrorist attack shattered the American sense of invulnerability – a fact that cannot be overstated – it is also true to say that on one level, perhaps even an unconscious level, television coverage of September 11 reproduced the horror of the threat of terrorism as a crisis of looking, a trauma of nothing to mourn.

To think about television's role in this event in this way is to shift the discussion of death and television away from the terms of the crisis of representation toward what Richard Terdiman calls 'the memory crisis'.[xvii] For Terdiman and other authors in memory studies, the crisis in representation of the kind I describe above is of social significance insofar as it leads to a situation in which people are cut off from the past. Memory, claims, Terdiman, is 'veiled in processes of commodification and reification', creating what Terdiman describes as 'an anxiety about forgetting' (12). He also claims that the memory crisis is anything but straightforward, taking the form of a tension between a concern that there is 'too little memory' and, at the same time, 'too much' (14). Television is the embodiment of this paradox. On one hand television is a constant source of faces of the dead in places such as Rwanda, Sarajevo and the Middle East, to name but a few. On the other hand the logics of speed and repetition that I have discussed throughout this book make these faces easily forgettable. We could say that the faces of the dead are re-called and endlessly repeated on news networks such as CNN, BBC and FOX, only to induce global forgetfulness.

In the aftermath of September 11, however, US networks especially (but also others in the West) responded to the crisis of nothing to mourn by undertaking a different kind of memory work, namely the work of memorialisation. This is of course the work Simonides undertook when he employed his good memory of spatial arrangement to make the dead recognisable. The West is familiar with scenes of 'the missing' in reports of the aftermath of war and terrorist acts in places such as Central and South America and the Middle East. Such faces, mostly black or non-white faces, are, as I suggested in chapter four seen through a different lens than that applied to the white face. This difference is accentuated in the television network coverage of the aftermath of September 11. Here, we see how Americans employed a number of different modes of cultural memory to fill the space of oblivion, the spatial and temporal void known as Ground Zero. Within hours of the event families and friends of the missing began posting photo portraits and family snaps on buildings in the vicinity. As they did so, television began transmitting these faces. In later days, these images, accompanied by personal information, such as mobile phone numbers, lists of family members' names, and so on, were plastered to the wire-mesh construction fence erected around the borders of the disaster zone. In the weeks and months that followed, the effort to identify the dead, to make them recognisable, extended beyond the fence. The *New York Times*, for example, took the unprecedented step of publishing long obituaries of 'the missing'. The publication of intimate details of the lives of everyday people transformed a space normally reserved for the recognition of public figures such as the rich, famous and powerful. This precedent in mainstream publishing is typical of the many ways in which September 11 not only constituted a global audience. It also served to further blur the increasingly unclear divide between the public and private spheres. In yet another unprecedented move, the American state undertook the extraordinary task of attempting to identify the remains of the more than 1500 people who remained 'missing' after the clearing of the Ground Zero site. This involved sifting through the recovered rubble for traces of bone and other human material that could be identified through DNA testing techniques and subsequently returned to victim's families. These state initiatives reveal the amazing divide in wealth and power between a nation such as America and countries where the state of emergency associated with terrorism is not the exception but the rule. It also reveals the extent of terror associated with the fear of 'nothing to mourn'.

IV: 'America Remembers'

In the months leading up to the first anniversary of September 11, the American state collaborated with community groups, families of victims and media networks to stage a mass mediated commemoration service of the victims of the disaster. The result was a global television event, titled 'America Remembers'. Three of Australia's commercial networks provided live, ad-free coverage, as did one of Australia's two state services. The remaining Australian commercial and state channels scheduled special programmes, such as news updates and/or documentaries on terrorist related subjects. In Australia, live coverage of 'America Remembers' did not rate as well as expected. The commemoration service itself was less popular than the melodramatic-style documentaries on the attack, such as *9/11*, which pre-publicity promised would show 'images never seen before'. Even in America, where ratings were strong, critical responses were mixed.[xviii] It is my guess that in Australia the event of 'American Remembers' was largely overshadowed by public concern about the imminent war in Iraq. On a cultural level, lack of interest could also be attributed to the fact that the commemorative rite of recalling the names of the dead – in this case, 2801 names – does not make for good television.

Most of the commercial networks that carried the live footage of 'America Remembers' added live commentary and pre-taped segments. This overlay of voices led to a number of ironic moments in the event that reveal the underlining contradictions in television as a form of public memory. In NBC's coverage, for example, a historian was asked to comment on the reading of the Gettysburg address at the opening of the memorial service. The host suggested that perhaps the reading of the names in this event 'replaces the bodies' present at the former. The historian agreed. She continued: 'I think it's a very moving thing to read the names, for what we see is that for these 2,800 people a whole circle of people surround them, and [the reading of the name] gives that moment of memory to them'. This may be true. But the fact is, news producers choose at this point to allow this comment and so many others throughout the coverage to drown out the reading of names, denying those people, their circle of friends, as well as viewers, 'a moment of memory'. This kind of thing occurred across the network broadcasts. Switching channels I learned from another commentator that a year later an estimated 1493 of those whose names were being read remain 'missing', meaning they remain unidentified, unrecognisable. In response, television reproduces the names of the faceless only to then efface them yet again. I would argue that as a form of public memory, the highly planned event 'America Remembers' sought to assure us as viewers that nothing goes away while, at the same time, reproducing the very processes of disappearance that it seeks to cover over.

Throughout this book I have tried to show how faces of death can turn to reveal what they conceal. On this occasion one face in particular struck me in this way. It is an image of a firefighter's father wearing a poster-size photographic portrait of his son around his neck in a bib-like fashion. Beside the image of his son's face were the words 'Remember Me', while along the bottom of the poster was his son's name – which I have since forgotten. I do remember, however, that when I was saw this particular image replayed several times in various reports of the anniversary of September 11, I felt in some way that it was already too late to remember this man's son. The particularity of this firefighter's death, which the father sought to draw attention to, is, I argue, erased, or *effaced*, as I would put it, the moment this image enters the field of television. Made visible in the thousands of replays all over the world, the face of this man's son became a generic image of September 11, appropriated into the larger mythic frame of death and nationalism. As such, this face is, surely, emblematic of a kind of facelessness television participates in every day of the week, a crisis in recognisability that demonstrates how public memory is always already shaped by social and historical contexts and, therefore, has no direct or unmediated relation to the past. Rather, as we see here, the past is always open to distortion and the power of myth. And in this regard, 'not even the dead', as Benjamin once warned, 'are safe'.[xix]

ENDNOTES

[i] Frances A. Yates, *The Art of Memory*, London: Routledge and Kegan Paul, 1966.

[ii] For an overview of literature on terrorism and media, see Kevin G Barnhurst, 'The Literature of Terrorism: Implications for Visual Communication' in *Media Coverage of Terrorism: Methods of Diffusion* ed. A Odasuo Alali and Kenoye Kelvin Eke (Newbury Park: Sage, 1991).

[iii] *The Age of Terrorism* (2002), written, directed and produced by John Blair. 3BM, Discovery.

[iv] Walter Laqueur, *The Age of Terrorism* (Boston and Toronto: Little, Brown and Company, 1987), 123.

[v] Martin Essler, *The Age of Television* (New Brunswick and London: Transaction Publishers, 2002. c.1982). Also see Brigitte Lebens Nacos, *Mass-mediated terrorism : the central role of the media in terrorism and counterterrorism* (Lanham, Md. : Rowman & Littlefield, 2002); Robert M. Batscha and others, *The Changing Dynamics of Terrorism on*

Television, University Satellite Seminar Series: Television and Terrorism; Part 1 & 2 (Los Angeles, CA.: Museum of Television and Radio, 1998); Grant Wardlaw, 'Terrorism and the Media: A Symbiotic Relationship' in *Political Terrorism: Theory, Tactics, and Countermeasures*, Second Edition (Cambridge University Press,1989; Michael Delli Carpini, 'Television and Terrorism', *Western Political Quarterly*, 40, March 1987, 45-64; Ronald D. Crelinstesn, 'Television and Terrorism: Implications for Crisis Management and Policy- Making', *Terrorism and Political Violence*, 9:4 Winter 1997, 8-32; John Carey, 'Media use during a crisis' in *Prometheus*, 20: 3, September 2002, 201-207.

[vi] Gaye Tuchman, *Making News: A Study in the Construction of Reality* (New York: Free Press, 1978), 49-58.

[vii] Menahem Blondheim and Tamar Liebes, 'Live Television's Disaster Marathon of September 11 and its Subversive Potential' in *Prometheus*, 20:3, 2002, 274.

[viii] On the relationship between disaster and live television, see Mary Anne Doane, 'Information, Crisis, Catastrophe' in *Logics of Television*, ed Patricia Mellencamp (London: British Film Institute, 1990) 222-239, and Daniel Dayan and Elihu Katz, *Media Events: The Live Broadcasting of History* (Cambridge Mass.: Harvard University Press, 1992); Philip Seib, *Going Live: Getting the News Right in a Real-Time, Online World* (Lanham, Md.: Rowan and Littlefield, 2002.

[ix] See Todd Gitlin, 'Embed or in bed? The war, the media and the truth' in *The American Prospect*, 14:6 June 2003, 42- 43.

[x] Kwami Karikari, 'I Wonder as I Wander: African Women Don't Cry', http://allafrica.com/stories/200109230069.html, as reprinted in paper for *Make World Festival*, Munich, Germany, 18-21 October, 2001, ed. Geert Lovnik, Sebastian Luetgert, Olia Lialina, et el.

[xi] Jonathan Flatley, '"All That is Solid Melts Into Air": Notes on the Logic of the Global Spectacle' in *Afterimage*, 30: 2, September-October, 2002, 1.

[xii] *9/11* (2002), directed by Jules and Gedeon Naudet, produced by CBS TV, distributed by Paramount.

[xiii] *9/11*, 2002.

[xiv] See W.J.T. Mitchell, '911: criticism and crisis (Editorial), Critical Inquiry, 28:2 2002, 567-573.

[xv] Jacques Derrida, 'No Apocalypse, Not Now (Full Speed Ahead, Seven Missiles, Seven Missives)' trans. C. Porter and P. Lewis, *Diacritics*, 14, 1984, 28.

[xvi] For an excellent collection of critical discussion on September 11, see *September 11: An Anniversary Issue (Social Text)*, ed. Ella Shohat, Stefano Herney, Randy Martin, et.al. (Durham: Duke University Press: 2002). Also see Jean Baudrillard, *The Spirit of Terrorism*, trans. Chris Turner (London: Verso 2002) and Christopher Hewitt, *Understanding Terrorism in America: From the Klan to Al Qaeda* (New York: Routledge, 2003).

[xvii] Richard Terdiman, *Present Past: Modernity and the Memory Crisis* (Ithaca, NY. and London: Cornell University Press, 1993).

[xviii] For a cross sample see Peter Johnson, 'Coverage of 9/11/02 was hard to criticize' *USA Today*, September 13, 2002; Tom Shales, 'Moving Pictures: on a day of remembrance, television puts itself in our place, *Washington Post*, September 12, 2002;

Joyce Purnick, 'A Modern-Rite of Mourning: Must See TV', *New York Times*, September 12, 2002; Steve Johnson, 'Difficult task marked by predictable excess', *Chicago Tribune* September 12, 2002; Staci Kramer, 'The Sept. 11 media frenzy', *Online Press Review*, September 12, 2002; Suzanne Ryan and Mark Jurkowitz, 'Networks struggle to fill time tastefully', *Boston Globe*, September 12 2002. (NB: These news articles and others can be easily accessed at *Daily Briefing: A Digest of Media News* @ Journalism.org.)

[xix] See Walter Benjamin, 'Theses on the Philosophy of History', *Illuminations*. ed. and intro. by Hannah Arendt, trans. Harry Zohn (London: Fontana, 1992).

Video enlargement from City Lights *(Author's collection)*

Chapter 7

First Sight: Blindness, Cinema and Unrequited Love

The romantic comedy *City Lights* (1931) is widely regarded as the most melancholy and most beautiful of Charlie Chaplin's films.[i] The story revolves around a tramp's love for a blind flower girl who mistakes him for a wealthy gentleman. The film's trope of 'blind love' provides the occasion for some of the cinema's most memorable sight gags. It also forms the basis of the film's critique of modernity and the cult of progress. In the course of the film the tramp rescues a suicidal, blind-drunk millionaire, who accepts him as a friend and drinking partner only to later reject him. As a social outcast, the tramp wanders city streets staring blindly at inanimate artefacts of modernity: war monuments, statues, shop dummies and other stony-faced objects that refuse to return his gaze. But the most significant blind-spot in this film occurs when the newly sighted flower girl sees the tramp for the first time only to fail to recognise him as her true love.

By way of ending this book I want to explore what I see as a certain kind of melancholy and trauma associated with this flower girls' shock of recognition, this instance of 'first sight' in which visual recognition comes too late. Taking a circuitous path through the spaces in between blindness and sightedness, love and loss, before returning full circle to the ending of *City Lights*, I explore the resonances between the phenomenon of blindness known as 'first sight' and Benjamin's idea of the dialectical image, characterised as simultaneous blindness and illumination.[ii]

I: 'Acting Like a Blind Man'

In 1930, just one year prior to the release of *City Lights*, the German psychologist M. von Senden published his influential study, *Space and Sight: The Perception of Space and Shape in the Congenitally Blind Before and After Operation*.[iii] An interpretive study of two centuries of research on the congenitally blind before and after operation, *Space and Sight* contributes to the theorization of space, while its purpose, the author writes, is to 'throw light on the full meaning of the task of teaching congenitally blind patients to see after operation' (14). It is an understatement to say that methods in this task have rapidly developed since this time. Nevertheless, von Senden's study of the state of being between blindness and sightedness remains of interest. It is a rich source book of studies of blindness in the eighteenth and nineteenth centuries. It also provides innovative interpretations of the processes of psychological transformation that patients undergo as they re-orient their perceptual life from one that has been predominately *tactual* to that which is now dominated by *visual* modes of perception. It also shows how a blind conception of space is not the same as it is for the sighted.

In *Space and Sight* von Senden reports that after operations to restore sight patients are likely to experience 'an initial stage of purely visual sensation', or what he calls an experience of 'first sight'. He offers this citation from the surgeon Grafe's (1891) case notes as a typical reaction:

> To begin with newly operated patients do not localize their visual impressions; they do not relate them to any point, either to the eye or to any surface, even a spherical one; they see colors much as we smell an odor of peat or varnish, which enfolds and intrudes upon us, but without occupying any specific form or extension in a more exactly definable way (129).

Von Senden interprets first sight as a sensory experience that bypasses or evades cognition. It is, he claims, 'a quite passive influx of visual impressions, which do nothing, as yet, to induce (the newly sighted patient) to emerge from his passive state' (130). He supports this claim with reference to a variety of historical case studies, such as the following observation by the French surgeon Marc-Monnier from the late nineteenth century:

> He [the newly sighted patient] does not know what he is seeing, and everything that vision tells us concerning lines, contours, proportions, distances and motions, is unknown to him.
> All his ideas were furnished by touch and hearing; those excited by the eye arrived too late; he took no interest at all in acquiring new knowledge; he continued to behave like a blind man.
> My own opinion is, that he never saw anything but a confusion, and that this was his own fault; that is why your world, as it appears to you, was and remained strange to him. All the images which delight your painter's eye flitted through his mind as a jumble of impressions, without his attention being drawn to them (133).

In a vein similar to von Senden's assumption about the passivity of the newly sighted, Marc-Monnier expresses his frustration with the fifteen-year-old male patient who, in his words, continues 'to behave like a blind man'. Marc-Monnier makes his view clear by opposing the newly sighted man's mode of perception to that of the painter. This conception of the 'painter's eye' attributed in a universal way to the sighted is premised on notions of pictorialism and perspectivism which assumes a viewer examines the image from a fixed point. 'Behaving like a blind man' is thus characterized as an inability to perceive 'inner order'- an experience of 'a jumble of impressions' with no fixed viewing position.

But is it only the newly sighted who behave this way? The experience of pure vision Marc-Monnier describes resonates strongly with Walter Benjamin's theorization of the child's perception of colour.[iv] In a fragment from his early writings, Benjamin claims that for the child 'colour is fluid and not a symptom (of form)' (51). It is, he says, 'a winged creature that flits from one form to the next' (51). In Benjamin's view the child's experience of colour is based not on a perception of form, but movement. And what is at stake, he argues, is a very specific relation to the world of objects. Here, 'colourfulness' is not perceived through perception of a spatial relation. Rather, it is constitutive of what he describes as 'a point of departure', that is, a perception of change. Whereas physicians like Marc Monnier conceive this lack of attention to form in the newly sighted as mental ineptitude, or, at the least, pathological passivity, Benjamin claims that the child's view of colour is nothing less than 'spiritual'. By this he does not mean anything religious but a process that, in his words, 'cancels out intellectual cross-referencing, without sacrificing the world' (51). Benjamin writes that the child's perception of colour represents 'the pure receptivity of the child', a state which, in his view, is lost to the adult. For according to Benjamin, the adult's task is to provide order and law, a fate that runs contrary to the work of the imagination:

> For the fact is that the imagination never engages with form, which is the concern of the law, but can only contemplate the living world from a human point of view creatively in feeling (51).

The 'human point of view', or, feeling, as Benjamin suggests, is activated in the child's imagination through perception of change. Or, to put it slightly differently, what adults lose in their role as lawmakers is a sensitivity or receptivity to change, to time. If there is common ground then between the vision of the newly-sighted who continues to behave like the blind and the child's view of colour it is not an indifference to the visual world but something much more specific, namely an indifference to form, to order. It is precisely these moments when the sight of the child's imagination is restored, when we become blinded to form and the law of order, that are of central concern to Benjamin's philosophy of the image.

In his most well-known essay, 'The Work of Art in the Age of Mechanical Reproduction', Benjamin questions the privileging of contemplation and absorption as proper modes of reception. He makes this comparison between film and painting:

> The painting invites the spectator to contemplation; before it the spectator can abandon himself to his associations. Before the movie frame he cannot do so. No sooner has his eye grasped a scene than it is already changed. It cannot be arrested. (Georges) Duhamel, who detests the film and knows nothing of its significance, though something of its structure, notes the circumstance as follows: 'I can no longer think what I want to think. My thoughts have been replaced by moving images'. The spectator's process of association in view of these images is indeed interrupted by their constant, sudden change. This constitutes the shock effect of the film, which like all shocks, should be cushioned by heightened presence of mind (231).

Here we see how for Benjamin, the film produces in the spectator precisely the lack of focus and heightened receptivity to tactile sensation Marc Monnier describes in his observation of his newly sighted patient. But unlike the surgeon, and, for that matter, other cultural critics at the time, such as Duhamel as well as his respected friend Theodor Adorno, Benjamin does not see distraction in negative terms. On the contrary, just as he finds something 'spiritual' in the child's perception of colour, so he argues that the distracted mode of being produced by the shock effect of film constitutes a potentially radical viewing position.

> The film is the art form that is in keeping with the increased threat to his life that modern man has to face. Man's need to expose himself to shock effects in his adjustment to the dangers threatening him. The film corresponds to profound changes in the apperceptive apparatus – changes that are experienced on an individual scale by the man in the street in big-city traffic, on a historical scale by every present-day citizen (243).

For Benjamin, film is not merely a modern art form. Rather, there is a structural reciprocity between the shock of modernity – the massive changes in temporal and spatial relations – and the constant, rapid shock effect of the film. Just as the 'first sight' of the newly sighted is a trauma in which visual sensation comes too soon, film can reveal the alienating conditions of modernity to the masses. Only, however, in its most shock producing forms, only as it constitutes a habitual way of responding.

II: A Space of Touch

The concept of habit is central to von Senden's study of blind modes of perception. Arguing for the specificity of blind perception of space, von Senden cites a well-known case of a fourteen-year-old blind and deaf boy recorded by the Scottish surgeon Wardrop in 1810. Wardrop reports that the blind and deaf boy had an unusual habit of creating circles with stones: '[T]he boy was observed to employ many hours in selecting from the channel of a river, which was near his father's house, small stones of a rounded shape, nearly of the same weight, and having smooth surfaces. These ... he would arrange in a circular form on the bank of the river, and place himself in the centre of the circle' (30). Wardrop argues that the boy's activity provides evidence of the child's ability to reproduce the shape of a circle formed in his mind's eye as a memory-image of spatial dimensions. In his discussion of the case, von Senden questions the orthodox conclusion that this memory-image is equivalent to sighted consciousness of a circle, arguing that this activity provides evidence of a consciousness of space peculiar to the blind that he calls 'a space of touch' based on the notion of 'touch-sequences' (32). Von Senden suggests that the boy's ring of stone is best understood as a 'circle from within', which corresponds to what he describes as the ultimate 'touch-sequence' of the blind: 'circle from without'. In other words, he is suggesting that the slow, methodical construction of the circle by the boy reproduces his most fundamental movement: the sequence of muscular sensations to his continuously controlling arms searching around him. He argues this activity constitutes a sort of schema 'containing not only the main features of the circle touch-sequence but also reference-points for the course of its completion' (32). In a long passage that is worth citing he claims that we are mistaken if we equate this schema with what the sighted understand as 'structure', for, in his words:

[w]hen as sighted persons we speak, for example, of the structure of a tree, we think too much in doing so of the spatial relationship of the parts to one another and to the whole; moreover, the possession of this spatial structure presupposes that we have previously experienced the tree as a whole. But this is precisely what the blind person has not acquired, and never can, even by the use of the schema ... Even when he is able, say, to finger all over a model tree and actually plant it in a tub, one still cannot say of him that he has thereby had a total experience of 'tree' as such. What he obtains from this is a series of qualitative impressions – extending from the gnarled texture of the roots to the twigs and leafage – and the temporal structure of change in these impressions, from root to trunk, branches, twigs and leaves. If he were to analyse these impressions more closely, he would be able to form a comparatively full schema of a 'tree', though it would continue to reproduce in compressed form the temporal structure of the perceptual process (32-33).

This idea of the image being constituted through 'the temporal structure of change in impressions' is a key point in von Senden's argument about the fundamental difference between blind and sighted perception of space. Certainly, the blind perception of space described here radically departs from the dominant theorization of space-perception which privileges spatial arrangement. But to what extent are these touch sequences, which von Senden argues form a temporal structure, indicators of a consciousness exclusive to the blind? If blind apprehension of the world is similar in process to the child's perception of colour, as I suggested earlier, it also has obvious correspondences to the experience of cinema. You could even say that the ability of the blind to build up an image through a succession of qualitative impressions of change is best described with reference to cinematic montage.

As we know, the cinematic image is formed through the rapid juxtaposition of fragmentary images unfolding in time. As with the images of the object world formed by the blind, the cinematic image appears only as it disappears; it is a *temporal* image. From the cinematic perspective the blind boy's placement of the stones can be seen not only as an enactment of the ultimate 'touch sequence of the blind', as von Senden suggests: it might also be read as a statement of the *montage* nature of blind modes of perception. The sighted routinely regard blindness as a perpetual state of spatial disorientation – being 'lost in the dark', so to speak. But if we take the blind boy's model of the fundamental process of blind perception as the formation of touch sequences – a compressed form of temporal structure – we can see that this mode of perception is not only about orienting oneself in space but a repetitive process of building images: the circle 'appears' only to disappear only to reappear. In this way, blind perception is similar to what Benjamin calls 'the shock effect of the film', a process of perception of 'constant, sudden change'.[V] Like cinema, blind perception is constituted through a series of tactile shocks. In this way, blind perception involves not only receptivity to sameness but also an acute awareness of change. In fact the boy's activity might be taken as a repeated *enactment* of the blind mode of perception as a material lesson in human organisation of shock: that is, his methodical laying out of the stones as a staging of the way in which we not only take in the world as a series of discontinuities but also how we manage these shock-rhythms by organising them into routine responses. This is not to say that habitual modes of reception can fully protect us from shock. Perhaps the boy knew all too well as he repeated the sequence that forms the circle of stones that shock inevitably breaks through the wall of habit, interrupting the flow. But as Benjamin understood, it is precisely these moments of interruption to normal modes of perception, moments in which we are temporarily blinded, that enable us to recognise the impossibility of grasping the world in its entirety. As with the blind boy, we learn from shock experience that there is no complete and lasting image.

III: Shock of Recognition

In the field of perception studies the face derives its special status from its conception as a unique pictorial experience.[vi] It is widely agreed by researchers in this area that recognizing faces is a more complex process than any other kind of pictorial recognition. One school of thought is that face recognition relies on a very restricted number of visual features and minimal differences in characteristics such as shape, texture, tone, and the relative positioning of facial features. Other researchers argue that recognition of the configuration of the features of the face is what makes the process difficult. But if perception of spatial arrangement is so fundamental to the process of face recognition, then how, we might ask, do blind people with their entirely different, temporal experience of space, recognise faces?

The image of blind 'face feeling' is, perhaps, the most clichéd of popular images of the blind. In addition to being demeaning, the image of blind people slowly, methodically feeling their way around the contours of a face is misleading. Here, again, von Senden's research on first sight is instructive. Take, for example, the surgeon Gayet's observation of a sixteen-year old, female patient who had regained her sight:

> I brought an uncle, of whom she was very fond, to sit by her bedside and told him to remain quite still; I stood behind him and told X to look at the face in front of her. 'That's your face', she said at once. 'Reach out for it then', I said. She stretched out her forefinger and ran it over a quite small surface of her uncles' cheek, and immediately her face beamed and she cried: 'It's my uncle!' (53).

Gayet's patient refuses to relinquish touch as her primary sense, and much to the surgeon's surprise, she continues to recognise faces by touch rather than by sight. In a similar case, von Senden reports that a newly sighted patient was 'confounded by the discovery that each new person who was brought in to see her had an entirely different face' (63). He adds, she had previously thought all faces were much alike except that some were rounder than others. If, as the young patient suggests, when she was blind she perceived all faces to be of a similar shape and form then, surely, it follows that she engages the sense of touch to perceive something *other* than the spatial dimensions of form, that is, the configuration of facial features. So what exactly is happening here? How does this blind girl recognise her uncle through just the briefest touch of a small section of his cheek?

To answer this question we need to rethink face recognition, which is normally thought of in terms of the *re*-cognition of a pictorial image already known: a conscious identification of the banal signs of individuation such as form, shape, the texture of skin (rough, smooth, with hair, without). Here, however, there is no evidence of face feeling, no suggestion that the girl methodically re-configures image-fragments of the face into a whole image, some kind of 'identikit' picture stored in her memory. Rather, judging by the temporal nature of this act of recognition – that is, the briefest of touches, the suddenness of her reaction – it would seem that the connection between the girl's finger and the small patch of her uncle's cheek takes the form of a small shock experience, a spark of some kind. As Gayet reported: 'Her face beamed and she cried, 'It's my uncle!'. Clearly, the girl is both surprised and pleased; suggesting that the connection formed in this instance through the sense of touch activates not the faculties of spatial re-cognition, but perhaps something closer to the phenomenon of involuntary memory (discussed earlier in chapter one). As with the child whose perception of colour 'cancels out intellectual cross-referencing', the sensation caused by the girl's bodily contact with her uncle's face seems to engage a receptivity to change, thus constituting a shock of recognition. What I mean by this is that the girl does not seem to recognise her uncle as 'a picture in her head' but rather she takes in his presence as a feeling, a tactual shock that sets off memories of him.

We might also consider the girl's recognition of her uncle as an act of 'facial vision'. The phenomenon of facial vision was first identified in 1749 by the French critic, Denis Diderot, in his well-known essay, 'A Letter About the Blind, For The Use of Those Who Can See'.[vii] Here, Diderot remarks on his blind acquaintance's amazing sensitivity, including his ability to perceive the presence of objects by sensing pressure or temperature changes on his face. He writes:

> (He) judges of his nearness to the fire by the heat, and of a vessel being full by the noise made when pouring liquid; and he judges of his nearness to objects by the action of the air on his face. He is so sensitive to the least changes in the currents of air that he can distinguish between a street and a closed alley.[viii]

Since Diderot's time, this hypothesised ability in the blind to sense the presence of objects through the face has been the subject of mystical explanations, ranging from dependency on magnetism to telepathy. More recently, the hypothesis has been overshadowed by the generally agreed upon understanding by researchers in this field that the primary mechanism of spatial perception in the blind is auditory. That is to say, blind people perceive the presence of objects by listening to the sounds of their own footsteps or vocalizations.[ix] But while this latter aspect of blind experience may well be the dominant mode of orientation, it does not follow that it invalidates blind perception of changes in air pressure and temperature on the face. As an instance of facial vision, the girl's recognition of her uncle is, again, similar to Benjamin's theorization of the child's perception of colour: a perception that 'enfolds and intrudes upon' the child. The girl's refusal to *see* her uncle's face, or, to put it more positively, her insistence on recognizing her uncle by the sense of touch can be understood not merely as resistance to sight, as is suggested by both Gayet and von Senden: it is, surely, also an act of determination to hold onto a specific mode of face recognition, one in which it would seem the face is experienced as a perception of change, a form of re-remembrance.

This conclusion accords with Benjamin's thinking on the shock experience of cinema. Benjamin saw cinematic techniques such as enlargement, microscopy, fragmentation and other forms of visual distortion, as shock-producing images that can jolt us out of habitual ways of seeing thus, allowing us not only to see the world anew. In this viewing position we can re-remember the past, that is, experience moments of what Benjamin calls 'recongnizability': instances in which the past is visible in the image of the Now that flashes before us, only to disappear. Like the cinematic image, then, the girl's recognition of her uncle's face is what Benjamin calls 'a dialectical image', a moment of recognition in which the past and present collide. It is, above all, a temporal mode of perception indebted to the sense of touch.

IV: In the World of Time

Clearly, the face takes on a very different shape and function in the world of the blind. Eyes also serve a different, tactual function. When Diderot asked his friend for his opinion of what he thought eyes were, the man replied: 'An organ on which the air has the effect this stick has on my hand'.[X] In these kinds of experience, the face is a tactile receptor of pressure changes in the air, of temperature, and other tactual forces. Blind experience of the face reminds us that face recognition is only one of the ways in which we identify others and are ourselves identified. It also reminds us that coming face-to-face with another involves senses other than sight. Just as the blind boy mentioned earlier re-remembers objects each time he encounters them through a touch-series, the shock of faces becoming unrecognisable in media culture can set off in the viewer forgotten memories of a tactile relation to the face. It does this not by shutting down the senses of sight and touch but, as the blind man of Puisaud once theorised might be possible, by 'making the contradiction between these two senses disappear' (250).

In chapter one I invoked one of my own childhood experiences of mortality – the act of reaching over to kiss my grandfather for the last time; an experience I remembered for the first time in the shock of the sight of actor Paul Eddington's apparent facelessness. This act of remembrance recalls the tactile relation children have to faces. Children feel their way around the contours of the faces of their primary carers', let's say, for example, their mother's face. Children routinely burrow their heads into the curve of their mother's neck, and they use their tongues to explore not only every object that comes their way, but that most precious object, the face of the mother. Toddlers are all mouth. It is an everyday occurrence for parents of a toddler to find themselves covered in the slobber of kisses and wet tongues that, for the child at least, constitute an experience of tactile, olfactory and gustatory delight. The same can of course be said of the exchange of affection between lovers. Levinas makes this point. But when he does, it is, as we saw earlier, part of a wider view of the ethical situation as a cancellation of the eyes. Here, I am making a different point. As I see it, the child's physiognomic perception of the face, that is, an everyday sense perception of the kind discussed in chapter two, is an experience in which sight and touch come together to open the eyes to the face as a particular practice of the image.

To be shocked into a remembrance of tactual experience of the face is entirely different to that other childhood experience of the face made famous in Jacques Lacan's formulation of 'The Mirror Phase.'[xi] In Lacan's psychoanalytic theory of the subject, self-alienation is based on a primary misrecognition by the subject of the Other as self. Lacan paints a scenario in which the face of the mother serves as a mirror in which the child mistakenly recognises his ideal self. This primary identification is thus founded not only on a misrecognition but also an idealisation of self. As Lacan and others, including Julia Kristeva tell it, the developing child is subsequently doomed to spend its life searching in the faces of others for that lost, ideal apparition of self.[xii] This conception of the face underpins theorisations of identity and identification in the cinema. But if we take a physiognomical point of view, we can see that the child's primary perceptual experience of the face need not take the form of an internalising gaze. You need only frown or smile a little too enthusiastically at a baby to make him or her cry with fear. And in this way, we could say that the child's perceptual experience of the inherent changeability of the face gives rise to a primary experience of the face as an image that appears only to disappear, is made only to be unmade, that is, an experience of change; an experience of time.

For now though, I simply want to make the point that this blinding shock experience of seeing faces appear only to disappear in the form of the changeability of all faces resonates with Benjamin's thinking on photo-media and time.[xiii] For Benjamin, the photographic image is like the name (as discussed in chapter four) in the sense that it is a mode of bereavement – it embodies the loss of the particular moment of its coming into being. Or as he puts it: 'Whatever we know will soon cease to exist, becomes an image.'[xiv] On this basis, blindness can be said to mark the point at which a thing disappears. It also marks the point at which a thing *becomes an* image. It seems to me that this simultaneous seeing and not seeing of the image rehearsed in the physiognomical sensation of the face is a form of blindness entirely different to that offered in Levinas' conception of the encounter with the other. In the first place, it does not lead to the subordination of the self. Unlike the demand of the face in Levinas' ethical situation, which as I argued in chapter one, inevitably becomes 'discourse', the demand for recognition I describe here is not a metaphor of death but the ground for which the face becomes a viable site for transmission of death. What I am suggesting is that we face death in the face of the other as a blind man faces the objects around him. Moreover, this awareness of mortality does not lead to questions of the 'inner life' but to the outer-world of others and things. Most importantly, it transports us, to use Proust's words, 'into a new world, that of time'.

This idea of blind perception as a sensitivity to change is, surely, the lesson Diderot hoped the sighted would learn when he addressed them with his account of the blind man of Puisaud's amazing capacity to see with/through his face. Or if we need yet another lesson from the blind we can turn to an extract from Dufau's study of a young blind girl, named Lucy (cited in von Senden's text), which allegorizes how perception of change is simultaneously tactual and visual. Determined to test the power of a sense she had only ever heard about, Lucy devised a series of experiments. The following is her account of her research into sightedness:

> I posed myself a host of questions about this new and unknown state which had been described to me, and did my best to come to terms with them. In order to satisfy my doubt, I had the idea of trying a strange experiment. One morning I again put on a dress which I had not worn for some time, because I had been growing so rapidly then from month to month, and thus attired I suddenly showed myself at the door of the anteroom in which my governess was already working at the window. I stood listening. 'Good Heavens, Lucy,' she said, 'why have you put on that old dress, that only reaches to your knees?' I merely uttered a few idle words and withdrew. This was enough to convince me that, without laying a hand upon me, Martha had immediately been able to recognize that I had again put on the dress that was too short. So this was seeing. I gradually recounted in my memory a multitude of things which must have been daily seen in the same fashion by the people about me and which could not have been known to them in any other way. I did not in the least understand how this happened, but I was at last persuaded. And this led gradually to a complete transformation of my ideas. I admitted to myself that there was in fact a highly important difference of organization between myself and other people; whereas I could make contact with them by touch and hearing, they were *bound to me* through an unknown sense, which entirely *surrounded me* even from a distance, *followed me* about, *penetrated through me* and somehow *held me* in its power from morning to night. What a strange power this was, to which I was subjected against my will, without, for my part, being able to exercise it over anyone at all. It made me shy and uneasy to begin with. I felt envious about it. It seemed to raise an impenetrable screen between society and myself. I felt unwillingly compelled to regard myself as an exceptional being, that had, as it were, to hide itself in order to live (61-62).

The image of Lucy hiding from the eyes of others might be taken as evidence of Levinas' view of the violence of the sense of sight. It is true, as Lucy says, sight not only brings the object closer, but in doing so, it allows the viewer to penetrate the object, in this case to 'penetrate through' the young girl. However, Lucy's account of her research into sight also reveals how this sense can *release* us, in the way that Kracauer uses the term when he claimed that it is precisely in the moments that film destabilises the notion of a unitary, impenetrable subject by making death visible that the spectator is released from 'the grip of consciousness'.[xv] Lucy reminds us how sight is a form of touch that binds us to the other. But just as one becomes an image, it is also the case that the image can penetrate the viewer, cutting through the veil of the illusion of a distinction between subject and object, self and other.

Here, Lucy learnt how it was possible to shock her governess by changing her image. Whether she was aware or not, she learnt how in becoming an image, a subject can penetrate another. This is what I have tried to show in this book. From the facelessness of actor Paul Eddington, to the television event of Dennis Potter's death, to the documentation of the racist de-facement of Eddie Mabo's grave and the image of Diana as 'forgotten Princess', we can see that although the face is employed throughout the image-cultures of contemporary media to conceal the powers of death, to cover over its terrifying unrecognisability, such faces can and do *turn* to reveal that concealment, to show the underside of the mask, to confront and penetrate the viewer.

V: The Face of the Beloved

In *One-Way Street* Benjamin reflects on what is possibly the most intense instance of facial vision: the face of the beloved.[xvi] He writes:

> He who loves is attached not only to the 'faults' of the beloved, not only to the whims and weaknesses of a woman. Wrinkles in the face, moles, shabby clothes, and a lopsided walk bind him more lastingly and relentlessly than any beauty. This has long been known. And why? If the theory is correct that feeling is not located in the head, that we sentiently experience a window, a cloud, a tree not in our brains but, rather, in the place where we see it, then we are, in looking at our beloved, too, outside of ourselves. But in a torment of tension and ravishment. Our feeling, dazzled, flutters like a flock of birds in the woman's radiance. And as birds seek refuge in the leafy recesses of a tree, feelings escape into the shaded wrinkles, the awkward movements and inconspicuous blemishes of the body we love, where they can lie low in safety. And no passer by would guess that it's just here, in what is defective and censurable, that the fleeting darts of adoration nestle (68).

As with the blind girl's recognition of her uncle's face, Benjamin's vivid description of the way in which the lover's feelings are released from the 'recesses' of the beloved's face confirms many of the ideas about the face as an image discussed in this book. Writing against the Platonic notion of ideal love, Benjamin proposes a non-transcendent form of the recognition of love, one that unsettles the distinction between subject and object. Here, feelings for the other reside in the lover's physical faults: 'wrinkles in the face, moles'. The face is not a mere sign – that is, a two-dimensional representation of the self – but a potential repository of past feeling, a storehouse, if you like. Moreover, as we saw with the blind girl's recognition of her uncle, feeling embedded in these features of the face at some past time can be *reactivated* in the present. For Benjamin, the experience of recognizing one's past feelings 'dazzled, flutter (ing) like a flock of birds' in the present takes us 'outside of ourselves'. It is a sentient experience that grounds us in a given place and time. Curiously, however, this experience of recognition is not, he suggests, entirely pleasurable. Rather, it is an experience that produces in the lover 'a torment of tension and ravishment'. For Benjamin, feelings of love are always crossed by a certain sense of melancholy and trauma. It is, I suggest, a form of recognition that can be best understood as the perspective of the unrequited lover.

In his *Moscow Diary*, Benjamin recounts an intimate occasion in which he reads the fragment quoted above from *One-Way Street* to his former lover Asja Lacis, to whom that book is dedicated.[xvii] It seems Lacis was as unmoved by the passage as she was by Benjamin's amorous advances. On one level, her lack of response to the piece is typical of her on and off again feelings for Benjamin over the years. More importantly, it offers some insight into the significance of unrequited love in Benjamin's philosophy of the image. In both the scenario he depicts in this fragment and his report on Lacis' response to it, Benjamin describes a very specific form of intimacy. As discussed in chapter four, the shock of recognition brings the lover into close proximity to his beloved, and yet, at the same time, puts him at an incommensurable distance to the one he loves, for his love remains a secret, 'undetected' by others. The unrequited lover is thus the figuration of Benjamin's messianic attitude: he or she who waits in hope for his or her feelings to be returned, that is for his or her love to be *recognised* by the beloved.

It is this image of the unrequited lover that leads us back to Chaplin's *City Lights*. Earlier I mentioned how the blind flower girl mistakenly took the tramp to be a wealthy gentleman. Throughout the film the tramp works hard to maintain the charade. In order to do this he must obtain a large sum of money to pay for an operation to restore the flower girl's sight. But the cost of this act of love is separation: the police mistakenly assume that the tramp stole the money given to him by the millionaire and he is sent to prison. Not knowing where her lover has gone, the newly sighted flower girl starts a new life, becoming a thoroughly modern business woman: a proprietor of a smart, new flower shop in a busy city centre. Yet, despite this successful assimilation into modern life, the flower girl continues to search for her lost love, until one day when, quite by chance, they cross paths.

When the girl first sees the tramp he is unrecognisable – a totally unfamiliar figure that she regards as an object of pity. In an act of charity she reaches out to offer the tramp a flower. This repetition of the gesture that originally brought the lovers together sparks a flash of recognition in the flower girl. As with the blind girl who recognises her uncle through the slightest touch of his cheek, the flower girl instantly recognises that the tramp is in fact her one true love. This shock of recognition is depicted in a series of close-ups, cutting back and forth between the lovers. What is revealed in the girl's face is that this image of her lover comes too late, a moment of recognition made all the more poignant by Chaplin's inspired decision to end the film on a close-up of the tramp nervously anticipating the girl's response.

It is often noted that Walter Benjamin was a great fan of Charlie Chaplin's films. In an unpublished commentary on Chaplin's parody of Hitler in *The Great Dictator* Benjamin claims that 'Chaplin has become the greatest comic because he has incorporated into himself the deepest fears of his contemporaries'.[xviii] How true! And following on from this we could say that the final close-up in *City Lights* generates a profound sense of melancholy not because we identify with the tramp but because, like the girl, we experience a shock of recognition. Just as the girl sees her lover's face for the first time only to recognise that this image comes too late, the unexpectedly abrupt ending in which Chaplin's unforgettable expression of hope appears only to disappear rehearses the forms of loss and trauma associated with modernity, that is, the impossibility of recovering 'what has become alienated and lost to human experience'. As with the blind girl who reaches out to touch her uncle's cheek, cinema's images of social change and the forms of loss peculiar to modernity come too soon. They are overwhelming, penetrating us 'much as we smell an odour of peat or varnish, enfolding and intruding upon us, but without occupying any specific form or extension in a more exactly definable way'.

ENDNOTES

[i] *City Lights: a comedy romance in pantomime*, written and directed by Charles Chaplin, United Artists, USA, 1931.

[ii] I am grateful to both Chris Healy and Ivor Indyk for their close reading of earlier versions of this chapter and their helpful suggestions.

[iii] M. von Senden, *Space and Sight: The Perception of Space and Shape in the Congenitally Blind Before and After Operation*, trans. Peter Heath (Glencoe, Illinois: The Free Press, 1960, C. 1930).

[iv] Walter Benjamin, 'A Child's View of Colour', *Walter Benjamin: Selected Writings, Vol 1, 1913-1926*, ed. Marcus Bullock and Michael W. Jennings (Cambridge, Mass. and London: Harvard University Press, 1996).

[v] For a critique of Benjamin's essay see, Miriam Hansen, 'Benjamin, Cinema and Experience: The Blue Flower in the Land of Technology', *New German Critique*, 40, 1987. On distraction, see Jodi Brooks, 'Between Contemplation and Distraction: Cinema, Obsession and Involuntary Memory' in *Kiss Me Deadly: Feminism and Cinema for the Moment* (Sydney: Power, 1995).

[vi] See, Hadyn D. Ellis and Andrew W. Young, 'Are faces special?' in *Handbook of Research on Face Processing*, ed. Andrew W. Young and Hadyn D. Ellis. Amsterdam: Elsevier Science Publishing, 1989.

[vii] Denis Diderot, 'A Letter About the Blind, For the Use of Those Who Can See', *Diderot's Thoughts On Art and Style*, trans. Beatrix L Tollemache (New York: Lennox Hill, 1971, C.1893).

[viii] Diderot, 'A Letter About the Blind, For the Use of Those Who Can See', 253.

[ix] For a standard text in this field see Bruce Goldstein, *Sensation and Perception*, 5th ed. (Belmont, Cal.: Wadsworth, 1984).

[x] Diderot, 'A Letter About the Blind, For the Use of Those Who Can See', 250-251.

[xi] Jacques Lacan, 'The mirror-stage as formative of the function of the "I" as revealed in psychoanalytic experience', *Écrits*, trans. Alan Sheridan-Smith (London: Tavistock, 1977).

[xii] See Julia Kristeva, *Black Sun: Depression and Melancholia*, trans. Leon S. Roudiez (New York: Columbia University Press, 1989). In this text, self-recognition is theorised as a recognition of the disappearance of self in the face/mirror of the departing mother. Hence, the subject is formed in what is according to Kristeva a primary experience of grief and loss.

[xiii] My understanding of this aspect of Benjamin's work is indebted to Jodi Brooks long standing work in this area. I am extremely grateful to Jodi for her intellectual generosity over the years and for the many helpful suggestions she has offered in regard to this project.

[xiv] As quoted and trans. in Eduardo Cadava, 'Words of Light: Theses on the Photography of History', *Fugitive Images: From Photography to Video*, ed. Patrice Petro (Bloomington and Indianapolis: Indiana University Press, 1995), 224.

xv Siegfried Kracauer, *Theory of Film: The Redemption of Physical Reality*, intro. Miriam Bratu Hansen (Princeton, New Jersey: Princeton University Press, 1997), 159.

xvi Walter Benjamin, 'One-Way Street', *Reflections: Essays, Aphorisms, Autobiographical Writings*, ed. Peter Demetz, trans. Edmund Jephcott (New York: Schoken, 1986.)

xvii Walter Benjamin, *Moscow Diary*, ed. Gary Smith, trans. Richard Sieburth (Cambridge Mass. and London: Harvard University Press, 1986),15.

xviii Walter Benjamin, 'Hitler's Diminished Masculinity', *Walter Benjamin: Selected Writings, Vol 2, 1927-1934*, ed. Michael W. Jennings, Howard Eiland, and Gary Smith (Cambridge, Mass. and London: Harvard University Press, 1996), 792.

REFERENCES

9/11 (2002). Directed by Jules and Gedeon Naudet. Produced by CBS TV. Distributed by Paramount.

Adorno, Theodor W. 'Cultural Criticism and Society'. In *Prisms*. Translated by Samuel Weber and Shierry Weber. London: Neville Spearman, 1967:19-34.

Alali, A. O., and Eke, K. K. *Media Coverage of Terrorism: Methods of Diffusion*. Newbury Park: Sage, 1991.

Arasse, Daniel. *The Guillotine and the Terror*. Translated by Christopher Miller. London: Allen Lane and Penguin, 1989.

Ariès, Philippe. *The Hour of Our Death*. Translated by Helen Weaver. New York: Alfred Knopf, 1981.

Aristotle. *De Anima (On the Soul)*. Translated by Hugh Lawson-Tancred. Harmondsworth: Penguin, 1986.

— . 'Physiognomics'. In *Minor Works*. Translated by W.S. Hett. London and Cambridge Mass.: William Heinemann and Harvard University Press, 1955.

Balázs, Béla. *Theory of the Film – Character and Growth of a New Art*. Translated by Edith Bone. New York: Dover Publications, 1970.

Barthes, Roland. 'The Face of Garbo'. In *Mythologies*. Translated by Annette Lavers. London: Paladin, 1973.

— . *Camera Lucida: Reflections on Photography*. Translated by Richard Howard. London: Vintage, 1993.

Batscha, Robert M. and others. *The Changing Dynamics of Terrorism on Television, University Satellite Seminar Series: Television and Terrorism; Part 1& 2*. Los Angeles, CA.: Museum of Television and Radio, 1998.

Bauman, Zygmunt. *Mortality, Immortality and Other Life Strategies*. Cambridge: Polity Press, 1992.

Beckett, Jeremy. 'The Murray Island land case and the problem of cultural continuity'. In *'Mabo' and Native Title: Origins and Institutional Implications*. Edited by W.S. Sanders, 7-24. Canberra: Centre for Aboriginal Economic Policy Research Australian National University, Research Monograph, No. 7. 1994.

111

Benjamin, Walter. 'A Child's View of Colour'. In *Walter Benjamin: Selected Writings, Vol 1, 1913-1926*. Edited by Marcus Bullock and Michael W. Jennings. Cambridge, Mass. and London: Harvard University Press, 1996.

— . 'Hitler's Diminished Masculinity'. In *Walter Benjamin: Selected Writings, Vol 2, 1927-1934*. Edited by Michael W. Jennings, Howard Eiland and Gary Smith. Cambridge, Mass. and London: Harvard University Press, 1996).

— . 'The Storyteller: Reflections on the Works of Nikolai Leskov', 'The Work of Art in the Age of Mechanical Reproduction', 'On Some Motifs in Baudelaire', 'Theses on the Philosophy of History'. In *Illuminations*. Edited and with an introduction by Hannah Arendt. Translated by Harry Zohn. London: Fontana, 1992.

—. '"N" (Re: the Theory of Knowledge, Theory of Progress)'. Translated by Leigh Hafrey and Richard Sieburth. In *Benjamin: Philosophy, Aesthetics, History*. Edited by Gary Smith. Chicago: University of Chicago Press, 1989.

—. 'Surrealism: The Last Snapshot of the European Intelligentsia', 'On Language as Such and the Language of Man', 'One-Way Street'. In *Reflections: Essays, Aphorisms, Autobiographical Writings*. Edited by Peter Demetz. Translated by Edmund Jephcott. New York: Schoken, 1986.

—. *Moscow Diary*. Edited by Gary Smith. Translated by Richard Sieburth. Cambridge Mass. and London: Harvard University Press, 1986.

— . 'A Small History of Photography'. In *One-Way Street and Other Writings*. Translated by Edmund Jephcott and Kingsley Shorter. London: New Left Books, 1979.

— . *The Origin of German Tragic Drama*. Translated by John Osborne. Introduction by George Steiner. London: Verso, 1977.

— . *Charles Baudelaire, A lyric Poet In The Era of High Capitalism*. Translated by Harry Zohn. London: Verso, 1973.

Blanchot, Maurice. *The Gaze of Orpheus and other literary essays*. Translated by Lydia Davis. Barrytown, NY: Station Hill, 1981.

Blondheim, Menahem and Tamar Liebes. 'Live Television's Disaster Marathon of September 11 and its Subversive Potential'. *Prometheus*, 20:3, 2002.

Bond, Anthony. 'Embodying the Real'. *BODY*. Sydney: The Art Gallery of New South Wales. 1997.

Brooks, Jodi. 'Worrying the Note': Mapping Time in the Gangsta Film', *Screen*, 42.4.

– References –

—. 'Performing Aging/Performance Crisis (for Norma Desmond, Margo Channing, Baby Jane, and Sister George)'. *Figuring Age: Women, Bodies, Generations*. Edited by Kathleen Woodward. Bloomington: Indiana UP, 1999.

—. 'Between Contemplation and Distraction: Cinema, Obsession and Involuntary Memory'. *Kiss Me Deadly: Feminism and Cinema for the Moment*. Sydney: Power, 1995. Bruss, Elizabeth. *Autobiographical Acts: The Changing Situation of a Literary Genre*. Baltimore: Johns Hopkins University Press, 1976.

Buck-Morss, Susan. *The Dialectics of Seeing: Walter Benjamin and the Arcades Project*. Cambridge, Massachusetts and London: MIT Press, 1995.

— . 'Aesthetics and Anaesthetics: Walter Benjamin=s Artwork Essay Reconsidered'. *October* 62 (1992): 3-41.

— . *The Origin of Negative Dialectics*. Hassocks: Harvester Press, 1977.

Bullock, Marcus. 'The Rose of Babylon: Walter Benjamin, Film Theory and the Technology of Memory'. *MLN* 103, no.5 (1988): 1099-1120.

Burke, Janine. *Joy Hester*. Elwood, Vic: Greenhouse, 1989.

Butler, Judith. *Excitable Speech – A Politics of the Performative*. Routledge: New York and London, 1997.

Cadava, Eduardo. 'Words of Light: Theses on the Photography of History'. In *Fugitive Images: From Photography to Video*. Edited by Patrice Petro. Bloomington and Indianapolis: Indiana University Press, 1995.

Capa, Robert. *Robert Capa*. Introduction by Jean Lacouture. Translated by Abigail Pollock. New York: Pantheon, 1989.

Carey, John. 'Media use during a crisis'. *Prometheus*, 20: 3, September (2002): 201-207.

Carpini, Michael, D. 'Television and Terrorism'. *Western Political Quarterly*, 40, March (1987): 45-64.

Chambers, Ross. 'Visitations: Operatic Quotation in Three AIDS Films'. *UTS Review* 2, no. 2 (1996): 24-67.

Clark, David ed. *The Sociology of Death: theory, culture, practice*. Oxford: Blackwell, 1993.

Collins, Felicity. *The Films of Gillian Armstrong*. The Moving Image Series, 6. St Kilda, Vic.: Australian Film Institute, 1999.

Cook, John. *Dennis Potter: A Life on Screen*. Manchester: Manchester University Press, 1995.

Coward, Rosalind. 'Dennis Potter and the question of the television author'. *Critical Quarterly* 24, no. 4 (1987): 79-87.

Cowlishaw, Gillian and Morris Barry (eds). *Race Matters: Indigenous Australians and 'Our' Society*. Canberra: Aboriginal Studies Press, 1997.

Creeber, Glen. *Dennis Potter Between Worlds: A Critical Reassessment*. Houndsmill, Basington, Hampshire and London: Macmillian Press, 1998.

Crelinstsen, Ronald D. 'Television and Terrorism: Implications for Crisis Management and Policy- Making'. *Terrorism and Political Violence*, 9:4 Winter (1997): 8-32.

Darwin, Charles. *The Expression and the Emotions in Man and Animals*. 3rd edn. Introduction and afterword by Paul Eckman. London: Harper Collins, 1998.

Davis, Therese. 'Becoming Unrecognisable'. *UTS Review* 4, no.1 (1998): 169-179.

— . 'The Face of a Saint'. In *Planet Diana*: *Cultural Studies and Global Mourning*. Edited by Re-Public, 93-96. Nepean, Sydney: Centre for Intercommunal Studies, 1997.

De Man, Paul. 'Auto-biography as De-facement'. *MLN* 94 (1979): 919-930.

Deleuze, Gilles. *Cinema 1: The Movement-Image*. Translated by Hugh Tomlinson and Barbara Habberjam. Minneapolis: University of Minnesota Press, 1989.

Deleuze, Gilles. *Foucault*. Translated by Seán Hand. Minneapolis: University of Minnesota Press, 1986.

Deleuze, Gilles, and Guattari, Fèlix. *A Thousand Plateaus: Capitalism and Schizophrenia*. Translated by Brain Massumi. Minneapolis: Minnesota University Press, 1987.

Derrida, Jacques. *The Gift of Death*. Translated by David Willis. Chicago and London: University of Chicago Press, 1995.

Derrida, Jacques. 'No Apocalypse, Not Now (Full Speed Ahead, Seven Missiles, Seven Missives)'. Translated by C. Porter and P. Lewis. *Diacritics*, 14 (1984).

Diamond, Hugh W. 'On The Application of Photography to the Physiognomic and Mental Phenomena of Insanity'. In *The Face of Madness: Hugh W. Diamond and the Origin of Psychiatric Photography*. Edited by Sander L. Gilman. Secaucus, New Jersey: Citadel, 1977.

– References –

Diderot, Denis. 'A Letter About The Blind For The Use of Those Who Can See'. In *Diderot's Thoughts On Art and Style*. Selected and translated by Beatrix L Tollemache. New York: Lennox Hill, 1971.

Doane, Mary Anne. 'Information, Crisis, Catastrophe'. *Logics of Television*. Edited by Patricia Mellencamp, 222-239. London: British Film Institute, 1990.

Eckman, Paul ed. *Darwin and Facial Expression: A Century of Research in Review*. New York: Academic Press and Harcourt, Brace, Jovanovich, 1973.

Erens, Patricia. 'Women's Documentary Filmmaking: The Personal is Political', *New Challenges in Documentary*. Edited by Alan Rosenthal, 554-65. Berkley: University of California Press, 1988.

Essler, Martin. *The Age of Television*. New Brunswick and London: Transaction Publishers, 2002. c.1982.

Flatley, Jonathan. '"All That is Solid Melts Into Air": Notes on the Logic of the Global Spectacle' in *AfterImage*, 30: 2, September-October, 2002, 1.

Freud, Sigmund. 'Slips of the Tongue'. In *The Psychopathology of Everyday Life, Vol. 5*. Edited by James Strachey with Angela Richards. Translated by Alan Tyson. Harmondsworth: Penguin, 1985.

Fuller, Graham ed. *Potter on Potter*. London and Boston: Faber and Faber, 1993.

Gage, John. 'Photographic Likeness'. In *Portraiture: Facing the Subject*. Edited by Joanna Woodall, 119-130. Manchester and New York: Manchester University Press, 1997.

Gilbert, Stephen W. *'Fight and Kick and Bite' – The Life and Work of Dennis Potter*. London: Hodder and Stoughton, 1995.

Gitlin, Todd. 'Embed or in bed? The war, the media and the truth'. *The American Prospect*, 14:6 June (2003): 42- 43.

Golden, James A. 'The Life and Death of Princess Diana: A British Philosophical/Rhetorical Perspective'. *Papers from An Era of Celebrity and Spectacle: The Global Rhetorical Phenomenon of the Death of Diana, Princess of Wales, A Trilogy of Conferences*. Edited by Gregory J. Payne. Boston: Centre for Ethics in Political and Health Communication, 2000.

Goldstein, Bruce. *Sensation and Perception*. 5th edn. Belmont, Ca: Wadsworth, 1984.

Gombrich, E. H. 'The Mask and the Face: The Perception of Physiognomic Likeness in

Life and Art'. *The Image and the Eye: Further studies in the psychology of pictorial representation*. London: Phaidon, 1982.

Goodwin, Sarah Webster. *Kitsch and Culture: The Dance of Death in Nineteenth-Century Literature and Graphic Arts*. New York: Garland, 1988.

Goodwin, Sarah Webster, and Elisabeth Bronfren eds. *Death and Representation*. Baltimore and London: Johns Hopkins University Press, 1993.

Goot, Murray, and Rowse, Tim eds. *Make A Better Offer: the politics of Mabo*. Leichhardt, NSW: Pluto, 1994.

Graham, Trevor. *Mabo: Life of an Island Man, Original Screenplay*. Sydney: Currency, 1999.

Gratten, Michelle ed. *Essays on Australian Reconciliation*. Melbourne: Black Inc, 2000.

Grigsby, Darcy Grimaldo. 'Dilemmas of Visibility: contemporary women artists' representations of female bodies'. In *The Female Body*. Edited by Laurence Goldstein, 83-100. Ann Arbor: University of Michigan Press, 1991.

Grosz, Elizabeth. 'Judaism and exile: the ethics of otherness'. *New Formations*, 12 (1990): 77-88.

Guillemin, Henri. *Joan, Maid of Orleans*. Translated by Harold J. Salemson. New York: Saturday Review Press, 1977.

Gunning, Tom. *D.W. Griffith and American Narrative Film*. Champaign: University of Illinois Press, 1991.

Gunning, Tom. 'In Your Face: Physiognomy, Photography, and the Gnostic Mission of Early Film', *Modernism/Modernity* 4.1, 1997: 1-29.

Hake, Sabine. 'Faces of Weimar Germany'. *The Image in Dispute: Art and Cinema in the Age of Photography*. Edited by Dudley Andrew. Austin: University of Texas Press, 1997.

Halliwell, Stephen. *Aristotle's Poetics*. London: Duckworth, 1986.

Hansen, Miriam. 'Benjamin, Cinema and Experience: "The Blue Flower in the Land of Technology"'. *New German Critique* 40 (1987): 179-224.

— . 'The Hieroglyph and The Whore: D.W. Griffith's *Intolerance*'. In *Classical Hollywood Narrative: The Paradigm Wars*. Edited by Jane Gaines, 169-202. Durham: Duke University Press, 1992.

– References –

— . '"With Skin and Hair": Kracauer's Theory of Film, Marseille, 1940'. *Critical Inquiry*, 19 (1993): 437-469.

Hegel, G. W. F. *Phenomenology of Spirit*. Translated by A. V. Miller. Oxford: Clarendon Press, 1977.

Hersey, George L. *Sexual Selection From the Medici Venus to the Incredible Hulk*. Cambridge, Massachusetts: MIT Press, 1996.

Jaggar, Alison M. 'Cultural Difference and Equal Dignity'. In *Hastings Center Report* (1994): 44-45.

Janes, Regina. 'Beheadings'. In *Death and Representation*. Edited by Sarah Webster Goodwin and Elizabeth Bronfen, 242-262. Baltimore and London: The Johns Hopkins University Press, 1993.

Jay, Martin. *The Denigration of Vision in Twentieth Century Thought*. Berkley: University of California Press, 1993.

Joyce, James. *A Portrait of the Artist as a Young Man*. Edited by Hans Walter Gabler with Walter Hettche. New York and London: Garland,1993.

Kayser, Wolfgang. *The Grotesque in Art and Literature*. Translated by Ulrich Weisstein. New York: McGraw-Hill, 1966.

Kearl, Michael C. *Endings: A Sociology of Death and Dying*. New York and Oxford: Oxford University Press, 1989.

Kellehear, Allan. *Dying of Cancer: The Final Year of a Life*. London, Paris, New York and Melbourne: Harwood, 1990.

Kirby, Lynne. 'Death and the Photographic Body'. In *Fugitive Images – From Photography to Video*. Edited by Patrice Petro, 72-84. Bloomington and Indianapolis: Indiana University Press, 1995.

Kinder, Marsha and Beverle Houston. *Close-Up: A Critical Perspective on Film*. New York: Harcourt, Brace, Jovanovich, 1972.

Koch, Gertrude. ' Béla Balázs: The Physiognomy of Things'. Translated by Miriam Hansen. *New German Critique* 40 (1987): 167-177.

Kostenbaum, Peter. *Is there an Answer to Death*? Englewood Cliffs: Prentice Hall, 1976.

Kracauer, Siegfried. *Theory of Film: The Redemption of Physical Reality*. Introduction by Miriam Bratu Hansen. Princeton, New Jersey: Princeton University Press, 1997.

— . 'Photography'. Translated by Thomas Y. Levin. *Critical Inquiry* 19 (1993): 421- 436.

Kristeva, Julia. *Black Sun: Depression and Melancholia*. Translated by Leon S. Roudiez. New York: Columbia University Press, 1989.

Kundera, Milan. 'Conversation with Milan Kundera on the Art of the Novel'. Translated by Linda Asher. *Salmagundi* 73 (1987): 119-135.

Lacan, Jacques. 'The mirror-stage as formative of the function of the I as revealed in psychoanalytic experience'. *Écrits*. Translated by Alan Sheridan-Smith. London: Tavistock, 1977.

Laqueur, Walter. *The Age of Terrorism*. Boston and Toronto: Little, Brown and Company, 1987).

Lavater, John Casper. [I]*Essays on Physiognomy*. 18th edn. Translated by Thomas Holcroft. London: Ward, Lock and Co.

LeBrun, Charles. *A method to learn to design the passions*. Los Angeles: William Andrews Clark Memorial Library and University of California, Los Angeles, 1980.

Levinas, Emmanuel. 'Ethics as First philosophy'. In *The Levinas Reader*. Edited by Sean Hand, 76-87. Oxford: Basil Blackwell, 1989.

— . *Totality and Infinity: An Essay on Exteriority*. Translated by Alphonso Lingis. The Hague, Boston and London: Martinus Nijhoff Publishers, 1979.

Levine, Susan Cohen. 'The Question of Faces: Special is in the Brain of the Beholder'. In *Handbook of Research on Face Processing*. Edited by Hadyn Ellis and Andrew W. Yound. Amsterdam: Elsevier Science Publishing, 1989. 37-48

Lingis, Alphonso. *Foreign Bodies*. New York: Routledge, 1994.

Lombroso, Cesare. *Crime, its causes and remedies*. Translated by Henry P. Horton. Montclair, New Jersey: Patterson Smith, 1968.

Loos, Noel, and Koiki Mabo. *Edward Koiki Mabo: his life and struggle for land rights*. St Lucia, Qld: University of Queensland Press, 1996.

Lovnik, G., Luetgert, S., Lialina, O., *et al*. Papers from *Make World Festival*, Munich, Germany, 18-21 October, 2001.

– References –

Mabo –The High Court Decision, Discussion Paper. Canberra: AGPS, 1993.

Magli, Patrizia. 'The Face and the Soul'. Translated by Ughetta Lubin. In *Fragments for a History of the Human Body, Part Two*. Edited by Michel Feher with Ramona Naddaff and Nadia Tazi, 87-127. New York and Cambridge, Mass.: Zone and MIT Press, 1989.

Maiorino, Giancarlo. *The Portrait of Eccentricity: Arcimboldo and the Mannerist Grotesque*, University Park, Pen. and London: Pennsylvannia State University Press, 1991.

Marshall, George N. *Facing Death and Grief : A Sensible Perspective for the Modern Person*. Buffalo, NY: Prometheus, 1981.

Marx, Karl. *The Economic and Philosophic Manuscripts of 1844*. Edited by D.J. Struik. New York: International Publishers, 1972.

Mellencamp, Patricia. 'TV Time and Catastrophe or *Beyond the Pleasure Principle* of Television'. In *Logics of Television*. Edited by Patricia Mellencamp. London: British Film Institute, 1990.

Mellor, Philip. 'Death in high modernity: the contemporary presence and absence of death'. In *The Sociology of Death: theory, culture, practice*. Edited by David Clark. Oxford: Blackwell, 1993.

Mellor, Philip and Chris Shilling. 'Modernity, Self-Identity and the Sequestration of Death', *Sociology*, 27, 1993.

Mitchell, W. J. T. '911: criticism and crisis' (Editorial), *Critical Inquiry*, 28:2 2002, 567-573.

Moller, David Wendell. *Confronting Death: Values, Institutions, and Human Mortality*. New York and Oxford: Oxford University Press, 1996.

Montagu, Jennifer. *The expression of the passions: the origin and influence of Charles Le Brun's Conférence sur l'expression générale*. New Haven: Yale University Press, 1994.

Morden, Terry. 'Documentary. Past. Future?'. In *Photography/Politics II*. Edited by Patricia Holland, Jo Spence and Simon Watney, 167-174. London: Comedia and Photography Workshop, 1986.

Nacos, Brigitte Lebens. *Mass-mediated terrorism : the central role of the media in terrorism and counterterrorism*. Lanham, Md.: Rowman & Littlefield, 2002.

Nash, Mark. *Dreyer*. London: BFI Publishing, 1977.

National Indigenous Working Group. *Native Title and Wik: The Indigenous Position:*

Coexistence, Negotiation and Certainty. Canberra: Aboriginal and Torres Straight Islander Commission and AGPS Press, 1997.

Neuberger, Julia. *Dying Well: A guide to enabling a good death.* Cheshire: Hochland and Hochland. 1999.

Olney, James. *Autobiography: Essays Theoretical and Critical.* Edited by James Olney. New York: Oxford University Press, 1980.

Ovid. *The Metamorphoses of Ovid.* Translated by Mary M. Innes. London: Penguin, 1995.

Payne, Gregory J., ed. *Papers from An Era of Celebrity and Spectacle: The Global Rhetorical Phenomenon of the Death of Diana, Princess of Wales, A Trilogy of Conferences.* Boston: Center for Ethics in Political and Health Communication, 2000.

Plato. *The Symposium.* Translated by Walter Hamilton. London: Penguin, 1951.

Rigby, Peter. *African Images: racism and the end of anthropology.* Oxford: Washington DC: Berg, 1996.

Ripstein, Arthur. 'Recognition and Cultural Membership'. *Dialogue* 34 (1995): 331-341.

Robbins, Jill. '*Visage, Figure*: Reading Levinas's *Totality and Infinity'. Yale French Studies,* 79 (1991): 135-149.

Scholem Gershom. 'Walter Benjamin and His Angel'. In *On Walter Benjamin: Critical Essays and Recollections.* Edited by Gray Smith, 51-89. Massachusetts and London: MIT Press, 1995.

Schopenhauer, Arthur. *Essays and Aphorisms.* Translated by R.J. Hollingdale. Harmondsworth: Penguin, 1970.

— . *The world as will and idea.* Translated by R. M. Haldane & J. Kem. London: Routledge & Kegan Paul, n.d.

Seale, Clive. *Constructing Death: The Sociology of Dying and Bereavement.* Cambridge, UK: Cambridge University Press, 1998.

Seib, Philip. *Going Live: Getting the News Right in a Real-Time, Online World.* Lanham, Md.: Rowan and Littlefield, 2002.

Sharp, Nonie. *No Ordinary Judgement – Mabo, The Murray Islanders' Land Case.* Canberra: Aboriginal Studies Press, 1996.

– References –

Simmel, George. 'The Aesthetic Significance Of The Face'. In *Essays, Philosophy and Aesthetics*. Edited by Kurt H. Wolff. New York: Harper Torchbooks, 1959.

Soloman, Maynard. Introduction to 'The Face of Man' by Béla Balázs. In *Marxism and Art: Essays Classic and Contemporary*, 281-288. Sussex: Harvester Press, 1979.

Tagg, John. *The Burden of Representation: essays on photographies and histories*. Basingstoke: Macmillian, 1988.

Taussig, Michael. *Defacement: Public Secrecy and the Labor of the Negative*. Stanford: Stanford University Press, 1999.

— . *The Magic of the State*. New York: Routledge, 1997.

— . *Mimesis and Alterity: A Particular History of the Senses*. New York: Routledge, 1993.

— . *Shamanism, Colonialism and the Wild Man*. Chicago and London: The University of Chicago Press, 1987.

Taylor, Charles. *Multiculturalism and 'The Politics of Recognition*. Commentary by Amy Guttman, Steven C. Rockefeller, Michael Walzer and Susan Wolf. Princeton: Princeton University Press, 1992.

Terdiman, Richard. *Present Past: Modernity and the Memory Crisis*. Ithaca, NY. and London: Cornell University Press, 1993.

The Age of Terrorism (2002). Written, directed and produced by John Blair. Distributed by 3BM/Discovery.

Tiedemann, Rolf. 'Dialectics at a Standstill: Approaches to the *Passagen-Werk*'. In *On Walter Benjamin, Critical Essays and Recollections*. Edited by Gary Smith, 260-291.Cambridge, Massachusetts and London: The MIT Press, 1995.

Tuchman, Gaye. *Making News: A Study in the Construction of Reality*. New York: Free Press, 1978: 49-58.

Von Senden, M. *Space and Sight: The Perception of Space and Shape in the Congenitally Blind Before and After Operation*. Translated by Peter Heath. Glencoe, Illinois: The Free Press, 1960.

Walter, Tony. *The Revival of Death*. London and New York: Routledge, 1994.

Wardlaw, Grant. *Political Terrorism: Theory, Tactics, and Countermeasures*. Second Edition. Cambridge University Press, 1989.

Warner, Marina. *Joan of Arc: The Image of Female Heroism*. London: Vintage, 1981.

Weinstein, Donald, and Rudolph M. Bell. *Saints and Society: Two Worlds of Western Christendom, 1000-1700*. Chicago and London: University of Chicago Press, 1984.

Williamson, Dugald. *Authorship and Criticism*. Sydney: Local Consumption Press, 1989.

Wyschogrod, Edith. *Saints and Postmodernism*. Chicago: University of Chicago Press, 1990.

Yates, Frances. A. *The Art of Memory*. London: Routledge and Kegan Paul, 1966.